CAMBRIDGE STUDIES IN CRIMINOLOGY, VOLUME XXX
Editor: Sir Leon Radzinowicz

LOCAL PRISONS: THE CRISIS IN THE ENGLISH PENAL SYSTEM

THE HEINEMANN LIBRARY OF CRIMINOLOGY
AND PENAL REFORM

CAMBRIDGE STUDIES IN CRIMINOLOGY

XX *Murder followed by Suicide*, D. J. West

XXI *Borstal Reassessed*, R. Hood

XXII *Crime in England and Wales*,
F. H. McClintock and N. H. Avison

XXIII *Delinquency in Girls*,
J. Cowie, V. Cowie and E. Slater

XXIV *The Police: a Study in Manpower*,
J. Martin and Gail Wilson

XXV *Present Conduct and Future Delinquency*, D. J. West

XXVI *Crime, Law and the Scholars*, G. O. Mueller

XXVII *Principles of Sentencing*, D. A. Thomas

XXVIII *Social Consequences of Conviction*,
J. Martin and D. Webster

XXIX *Suspended Sentence*, M. Ancel

XXX *Local Prisons: the Crisis in the English Penal System*,
R. F. Sparks

LOCAL PRISONS: THE CRISIS IN THE ENGLISH PENAL SYSTEM

by

Richard F. Sparks
Assistant Director of Research
Cambridge Institute of Criminology

HEINEMANN
LONDON

Heinemann Educational Books Ltd

LONDON EDINBURGH MELBOURNE TORONTO
SINGAPORE JOHANNESBURG HONG KONG
AUCKLAND IBADAN NAIROBI NEW DELHI

ISBN 0 435 82870 3

First published 1971

Publisher's note: This series is continuous with the Cambridge Studies in Criminology, Volumes I to XIX, published by Macmillan & Co., London

Published by Heinemann Educational Books Ltd
48 Charles Street, London W1X 8AH

Printed in Great Britain by
Morrison and Gibb Ltd
London and Edinburgh

Foreword

by Sir Leon Radzinowicz

The prison system is passing through a grave crisis, a crisis of overcrowding. There are far too many customers for far too few places. Anyone with the slightest knowledge of prison organization will know what this means, both for prisoners and for staff. And the crisis has by no means reached its peak yet. Things will get much worse before they become slightly better.

Dr Sparks has turned a searchlight upon this predicament at its most acute: in the local prisons. In spite of all the new institutions that have been built, those still represent the bread and butter of confinement. As theft is to crime, so are they to the penal system, giving it its shape and its physiognomy.

In 1938 I said that the English prison yielded place to none, that in many respects it surpassed those to be found anywhere else. I could not say that today. And even then, though much had been done to eliminate squalor and moral contamination, there was an absence of positive purpose. At best the prisons were neutral. They lacked ruthlessness but also moral vigour. It was hard to tell whether their effects were bad or merely indifferent.[1]

At that time the great movement, begun in 1907 and summed up by the Webbs as reforming prisons by keeping people out of them, was still accomplishing miracles. It was abetted by the fact that, although crime was already going up, its more serious forms were not greatly increasing.

Those good days are gone. There are limits to what alternatives to prison can do for us now. So we have our backs to the wall.

Dr Sparks has examined all this in the microcosm of a single prison—Winson Green, Birmingham. This detracts nothing from the wider significance of his analysis. Quite the contrary: it gives it the solidity of a real situation.

The terseness, the nervous rhythm, of this small book, carries the reader along—and it should have many readers.

Cambridge
February 1971

[1] See Leon Radzinowicz, 'The English Prison System' and 'The Assessment of Punishments by English Courts', both reproduced in *The Modern Approach to Criminal Law* (1945), pp. 123 and 110.

Table of Contents

Preface

The research described in this book was conceived and begun in the latter half of 1966. The Royal Commission on the Penal System was still in existence at that time; and it had been planned to carry out, for the use of the Commission, a survey of a 15 per cent sample of the total prison population of England and Wales on a single day. Staff and students in a number of universities agreed to collect the appropriate information from prisons, and Dr Winifred Cavenagh and I were asked to be responsible for its collection from prisons in the Birmingham area.[1] Before this could be done, the Royal Commission was dissolved, and the total population survey had to be abandoned. But in view of the limited information available on the population of the prison system, the idea of a descriptive survey still seemed a good one; accordingly, Dr Cavenagh and I approached the Home Office and were given facilities and financial support to carry out such a survey at Winson Green Prison in Birmingham, using a 25 per cent sampling fraction instead of the 15 per cent fraction originally envisaged.

As the work progressed, it became clear to me that, though the general local prisons are important both because of their size and because of the enormous penological problems they present, still they could not be meaningfully studied in isolation from the rest of the English prison system. Moreover, it was clear that the population and the problems of the general locals are in part a consequence of their place in the prison system, and of their relations both with other types of institution and with the rest of the penal system. The focus of the research was accordingly widened, to include (so far as possible) the whole of the prison system, and the movement of prisoners within it, as well as the population of one sector of that system. In recent years there has been an increasing amount of research on the operation of social and economic systems of various kinds; but little work of this kind has yet been done in the crimino-

[1] At that time, I was Lecturer in Criminal Law and Criminology in the Faculty of Law, and Dr Cavenagh was Senior Lecturer in Social Studies in the Faculty of Commerce and Social Science, at the University of Birmingham.

logical and penological fields. This book does no more than make a start; hopefully, however, the subject will receive more attention in the future.

Our research met with a number of delays, owing to unfortunate periods of illness among our staff, to some unforeseen difficulties encountered in data collection, and to my own move from Birmingham to Cambridge late in 1967. But despite these delays, and developments in the prison system since 1966, the results of our research are still topical. As the recent White Paper *People in Prison*[1] makes clear, the present condition of the English prison system is in many ways critical. It was estimated in this White Paper that the numbers in custody, in all types of establishment, would rise to over 40,000 in the next few years; in fact, this number was exceeded in July 1970.[2] The Government has already announced its intention to invest more money in prisons in this period. But in addition to the provision of resources, the prison system needs new ideas; there is a need to consider priorities among the many objectives of the system, and to find the best ways of accomplishing those objectives. To do this, much more knowledge is needed about prisons, about the men incarcerated in them, the men who staff them, and the social system in which prisoners and staff alike live while in the institution. This book makes only a very modest contribution to that knowledge. But it does, I hope, at least clarify some of the issues involved.

The final analysis of the data from our research, and the writing of this report, are entirely my work. I must accept full responsibility for any errors, omissions or misstatements. But the research owes an enormous amount to Dr Cavenagh's efforts in the planning and data collection stages; and I am deeply indebted to her for the helpful comments which she made on the final manuscript, as well as for her encouragement throughout the research. Great credit must also go to our principal research assistant, Mrs Nora Wilkins, who coped heroically with the collection of information from a wide range of agencies and who was solely responsible for obtaining all of the data on the sample of 1963 receptions. We also had the help, for more limited periods, of Joyce Bennett, Ann Giles, Marjorie Hankin, Jill Storey and Neil Thomas, in interviewing prisoners and extracting data from records. Normally I detest the use of the first-person plural by solitary authors. But I have nonetheless written 'we'

[1] Cmnd. 4214 (London: HMSO, 1969).
[2] Ibid., p. 104; see also pp. 91, 136 below.

instead of 'I' in many places in this book; this is not a lapse from principles, merely an inadequate recognition of my colleagues' contribution to the project.

My sincere thanks are also due to the Governor of Winson Green prison, Mr A. C. Packham, OBE, and to all of the staff of the prison who co-operated in making our research possible, during a busy and difficult time in the life of the institution; and to those members of staff at other prisons which we visited in order to interview the inmates in our sample. Special thanks are due to Mr K. Shirley, administrative officer in charge of the discipline office at Winson Green, for his patient assistance in uncovering information which we needed.

I am grateful to Mr T. S. Lodge, CBE, Statistical Adviser and Director of Research at the Home Office, and to his colleagues Dr Charlotte Banks, Mr S. G. Clarke, and Mr A. Weatherhead; all of them made many helpful comments on the manuscript, and saved me from several mistakes. I am also indebted to Professor Sir Leon Radzinowicz for much valuable editorial advice. The responsibility for any remaining errors in the book is, of course, mine alone; and the opinions expressed, and the conclusions reached, do not necessarily represent the views either of the Home Office or of any of the persons just mentioned.

Finally, I must acknowledge the help of my wife, Jennifer, who not only put up with the whole project but also assisted in the later and duller stages of the work, thereby learning a good deal more about prisons and prisoners than she really wanted to know.

R.F.S.

I

Introduction

The prison system of England and Wales is now undergoing a number of rapid and potentially far-reaching changes. After a lengthy period of comparative neglect, the prisons are receiving the attention of Parliament, penal reformers and the general public. Important changes in the system were introduced by the Criminal Justice Act 1967,[1] and in a White Paper[2] published late in 1969, the Government announced a substantial programme of capital investment in new prisons and the renovation of existing buildings, which will be carried out over the next few years.[3]

The main cause of this interest is undoubtedly the steady increase in the number of men in prison which has taken place in recent years. Though the total number of persons in custody in prison service establishments (prisons, borstals, detention centres and remand centres) declined slightly in 1968, after the Criminal Justice Act 1967 came into force, it rose again in 1969, and had reached over 35,000 by the middle of that year;[4] it rose even more sharply in 1970, and it seems clear that it is likely to continue to increase still further in the next few years. At the same time, the regime of the prisons has been affected to some extent by the changes recommended in the Mountbatten report[5] on prison escapes and security; and the abolition of capital punishment, and the rise in numbers of very long prison sentences for robbery and certain other offences, have focussed official attention on the problem of the long-term prisoner.[6] But while it is generally agreed that further changes in the prison system are necessary, the nature of these changes is not agreed; and

[1] 1967, ch. 80, esp. ss. 37–50, 59–64; see below, pp. 75–85.

[2] *People in Prison*, Cmnd. 4214 (London: HMSO, 1969).

[3] Ibid., paras 183–196.

[4] See the Report of the Prison Department for 1968, Cmnd. 4186 of 1969, note to p. 1. These reports will henceforth be cited as RPD, followed by the year to which the report being cited refers, in parentheses; the report of the Prison Commission (which became the Prison Department in 1964) will be similarly cited as RPC; and the separate volumes of statistical tables published by the Department since 1964 will be similarly cited as RPDS.

[5] See Lord Mountbatten's report on prison escapes and security, Cmnd. 3175 (London: HMSO, 1966), esp. paras 14–23.

[6] *The Regime for Long-Term Prisoners in Conditions of Maximum Security*, a report of the Advisory Council on the Penal System (London: HMSO, 1968).

indeed, the alternatives are at present very far from clear. Unfortunately there has been very little research carried out to date in England, on the effectiveness of imprisonment of different types in reforming different types of offender.[1] Very little is known about the English prisoner's experience of incarceration, and the relations between this experience and post-prison behaviour. Without more information of this kind, any conclusions as to the proper place of imprisonment in the English penal system can only be provisional.

Problems which cannot be solved, however, may at least be accurately identified and defined. The purpose of this book, therefore, is to describe the English prison system,[2] and to summarize, in brief and fairly general terms, what is known about some of the inmates of that system. Special attention will be paid to two aspects of the subject which seem to me to have been relatively neglected up to now. The first of these is the interrelationships between the different types of institution which make up the prison system, and between those institutions as a group and the rest of the penal system (including the courts and the police). The sixty-odd prisons which now contain adult males under sentence for criminal offences do not function completely independently of one another. Instead, they are linked together by a fairly definite set of administrative policies, according to which prisoners are transferred from one type of institution to another. Some of these policies are formally defined, by statute, statutory instrument, or standing orders; others may be defined less formally, by prison governors or other administrators. These policies are influenced by a number of different factors, and may change over time in response to external pressures on the system (such as public concern over security) as well as through internal changes (e.g. in institutional regimes). Moreover, even in the short run they have had to be modified or departed from because of physical factors such as overcrowding or staff shortages. Nonetheless, at any point in time they can in principle be identified with

[1] Cf. the Eleventh Report from the Estimates Committee, together with minutes of evidence taken before the Sub-Committee on Social Affairs, Session 1966–67: Prisons, Borstals and Detention Centres, H.C. 599 (London: HMSO, 1967), paras 196–199. Some data on the relative 'effectiveness' of imprisonment, and on factors associated with reconviction after imprisonment, are provided by a few recent studies: see, e.g., *The Sentence of the Court, A Handbook for Sentencers* (London: HMSO, 2nd ed., 1969), part VI; C. Blackler, 'Primary Recidivism in Adult Men: Differences Between Men on First and Second Prison Sentences', (1968) 8 *Brit.J.Criminol.* 130.

[2] From now on, references to England will include Wales unless the contrary is stated.

some precision; and in practice, in the case of the English prison system, they have in fact been fairly stable over the past few years. It is these interrelationships which justify us in speaking of a prison *system*, as opposed to a collection of similar institutions.[1] The men received into prison under sentence in any period of time—a year, say—are the system's *input*; those in prison at any time may be termed the system's *population*; those discharged are the system's *output*, some portion of which will return to the system as its input in the same or future years.

In a similar fashion, the prisons are linked, by the courts, to other types of penal measures. Again, some of these connections are specified by statute, or statutory instrument: the most obvious examples of these are the rules relating to measures for offenders aged under 21.[2] But in addition, within this framework of statutory limitations, there exists a large body of sentencing policies and practices designed to regulate the allocation by the courts of offenders to different penal measures.[3] Thus we may speak of the penal *system*, within which the prisons, young offenders' institutions, etc., function as linked sub-systems connected by the courts. We may trace the operation of this system back still further, and include the police, who first apprehend certain offenders, and who then decide whether to prosecute them in court, or merely caution them (formally or informally).

Offenders, once detected, enter this system; if prosecuted and convicted, they are allocated to some type of penal measure; and after some time—it may of course be a very short time—most are discharged from the system and re-enter the general population. Of the ex-offenders in the general population, a fraction are apprehended

[1] Cf. *OED*, s.v. 'system': an organized or connected group of objects; a set of things connected, associated or interdependent, so as to form a complex unity; a whole composed of parts in orderly arrangement according to some scheme or plan.

[2] See, for example, Criminal Justice Act 1948, ss. 17–20; Criminal Justice Act 1961, ss. 1–10; Children and Young Persons Act, 1933, Parts III and IV; and when implemented, Children and Young Persons Act 1969, ss. 1–7. There are also some direct connections provided by statute between some of these measures; see, for example, Criminal Justice Act 1948, s. 72, which provides that an unruly person in an approved school may be transferred by a court to a borstal institution even though he has not been convicted of another crime. In addition, the borstals and approved schools (but not detention centres or attendance centres) have well-defined internal allocation policies.

[3] For a recent discussion of these policies in relation to the higher courts in England, see D. A. Thomas, *Principles of Sentencing* (London: Heinemann, 1970); and below, pp. 59, 78–79.

again, and re-enter the penal system as recidivists; and smaller fractions pass through the system several times during their lives. In a system containing *n* different measures, there are in theory n^2 possible transitions between measures which the recidivist offender may make at each successive conviction; that is, there are n^2 possible paths between his last measure and his current one, which he may take within the system, each time he passes through it. As we shall see,[1] however, the paths which recidivists generally take, in practice, on successive convictions are fewer in number than this; and they are in fact fairly predictable.

Those offenders apprehended more than once in their lives—who at some time are part of the output of one sector of the penal system—thus constitute part of the input of the penal system at some later time. In this respect, the penal system resembles many other systems: for example, the educational system, in which part of the output of one sector (e.g. the primary schools) also becomes part of the input of another sector (e.g. the universities) at some later time. There are, of course, many important differences between these two systems. Not the least of these is the fact that those who stay in the educational system are by and large the system's 'successes'; that is, those who are willing and able to continue into further education. Those who stay in (or return to) the penal system, on the other hand, are in some sense the system's 'failures', since a general objective of the system is to reform or deter from crime those who get caught up in it. Nonetheless, the two systems, *qua* systems, are in many respects similar. The penal system may also be likened to the economic system, in which industries manufacturing different products buy from and sell to one another, as well as selling to final consumers. From this point of view the police, courts, prisons, and so on, can be regarded as processes for turning first, second, etc. offenders into second, third, etc. offenders, who are then returned to the general population; at each step, a portion of this output is finally 'consumed' either by becoming 'reformed' or by dying, emigrating, or becoming otherwise removed from risk of further reconviction. Again, there are many obvious differences between the two systems; but there are also structural similarities, which it may be useful to bear in mind for the purposes of penal policy.

It follows from the interrelationships between the different parts of the penal system, that changes in the operation of any one part

[1] Below, pp. 21–23.

may have important effects on the other parts. Thus in planning changes in any part of the penal system—in the prison system, for example, or young offenders' institutions—it is important to bear in mind not only the likely consequences for the part being changed, but also what may happen to other parts which are connected with it. Otherwise, a gain in effectiveness at one point may be more than offset by a decrease in effectiveness elsewhere. Moreover, in purely economic terms, not only of money but of manpower, the different parts of the penal system must to some extent compete for limited resources.[1] An optimum policy for the penal system as a whole may entail a very different policy concerning prisons, say, than would be suggested by considering the prisons in isolation. One objective of this book, then, is to describe some of the connections between the different types of institution which now make up the English prison system and the connections between those institutions and the rest of the English penal system. The development of mathematical models of these two systems is now in progress; a brief account of this ongoing work, and of related work in other fields, is given in Appendix A.[2]

The second main objective of this book is to describe one sector of the English prison system—namely, the general local prisons—and the population of men serving sentences in those prisons for criminal offences. Surprisingly little is known about the men who constitute the prison population. There have been a few surveys in the past of the populations of particular prisons, and studies of particular types of prisoner[3]; but for various reasons none of these

[1] I am not suggesting, of course, that economic costs are the only or even the most important ones to be taken into account by a rational penal policy; merely that they are one factor which must be considered. It is furthermore important to note that in purely economic terms the penal system must compete for resources with the health service, child care, and other branches of the social and welfare services; and that to an unknown (but possibly important) extent the functions and the clientele of these services overlap with those of the penal system.

[2] Below, pp. 112–124.

[3] The best of these is in T. and P. Morris, *Pentonville* (London: Routledge, 1963), chapter 3. The authors carried out a census of the total Pentonville population on 30 September 1959. Apart from its date, however, this study is of limited value for present purposes since Pentonville is (or was in 1959) a prison exclusively for recidivists, almost all of whom had served at least one previous prison sentence. In addition, London prisons differ in several ways from those in other parts of the country. The earlier study by W. F. Roper, 'A Comparative Survey of the Wakefield Prison population in 1948 and 1949', (1950) 1 *Brit. J. Delinq.* 15, 243, has similar limitations. A more recent study of female prisoners is N. Goodman and J. Price, 'A description of women in prison on January 1, 1965', in *Studies of Female Offenders, Studies in the Causes of Delinquency and the*

provides a detailed and up-to-date factual picture of the men in any type of institution in the English prison system, or in the system as a whole. The Prison Department of the Home Office publishes some statistical information each year on receptions into prison, but these statistics, though markedly improved in both scope and accuracy in recent years, are still limited in many respects. They provide a very broad picture of prisoners' previous criminality and penal careers; but they give no information at all about the prisoners' social backgrounds, family circumstances, etc. In any case, statistics of *receptions* into prison—that is, of the prisons' input—can give very little information by themselves about the prison *population*, since this is a function not only of the types of men received but also of the lengths of sentences which they serve. The majority of men received into prison in any year are serving fairly short sentences; in 1967, for example, over 70 per cent were under sentence of six months or less. But the system's population looks very different; short-sentence men form a much smaller fraction of those incarcerated at any time, simply because they pass through the system so quickly. There are, as we shall see, considerable differences in the current offences of men serving sentences of different lengths; and there are some other important differences as well. These must be borne in mind for the purposes of planning and administration. For example, the types of work which can be done in prison will depend primarily on the work skills of the average population, whereas after-care needs are related to men discharged from prison, i.e. to a lagged function of receptions. The contrast between receptions and population is also important in relation to the study of the informal social system of the prison, since it is reasonable to suppose that the development of relationships among inmates, and between inmates and staff, are influenced by the amount of time in which they are in contact with each other.

As we shall see, the population of the general local prisons is not representative of the whole of the English prison population, owing to the allocation policies used within the system, by which prisoners of certain types are transferred to other types of institution for part of their sentences. But all prisoners begin their sentences in general local prisons; and at any time these institutions contain almost half

Treatment of Offenders (London: HMSO 1967, 63–78). See also D. Clemmer, *The Prison Community* (1958 ed.) chap. 4, for a population survey of an American institution; and P. Morris, *Prisoners and Their Families* (London: Allen and Unwin, 1965), for a study of married prisoners in England.

of the adult male population of prisoners under sentence. In quantitative terms alone, then, they are an important sector of the system. Moreover, at the present time the local prisons present some of the most acute penological problems of the English prison system. They are grossly over-crowded, and the bulk of their clientele are serving fairly short sentences; most of them are over a hundred years old, and in physical terms they are far from ideal. Moreover, they are multi-functional institutions, since they must cope with men on remand awaiting trial or sentence as well as with men serving sentences; and their population is an extremely heterogeneous one.

My description of the population of these prisons is based mainly on a survey of a sample of the population of one large local prison—Winson Green, in Birmingham—which was begun at the end of 1966. Information concerning the 167 men in this sample—who comprised 25 per cent of the prison's population on the day when the research was begun (26 September 1966) was collected from prison records, from the police, probation records, and other social agencies, as well as (in most cases) from the men themselves.[1] By this method it was possible to overcome many of the deficiencies of existing prison records, and to assemble a fairly detailed picture of the social backgrounds, as well as the previous criminal and penal histories, of the men. In addition, more limited data were collected on a random sample of receptions into Winson Green in 1966; and on receptions into the same prison in 1963. These data throw some light on allocation and transfer policies within the prison system, and thus make possible some rough estimates of the composition of other types of prison.

The plan of the rest of this book is as follows. Chapter II deals with the present structure of the English prison system; it describes the types of institutions which the system now contains, and the policies which—at least until recently—have governed transfers of prisoners of various types between these institutions. This chapter also summarizes the relations between the prison system and other types of measures, which make up the penal system for adults, and describes the consequences of these relations for the input of the prison system. Chapter III deals with the population of the local prisons, and presents the results of the surveys carried out at Winson Green. Chapter IV is concerned with the composition of the

[1] The methodology of this research is briefly described in Appendix B, pp. 125–131 below.

populations of other types of prison, and with the implications of the differences which appear to exist between these institutions. Survey data (comparable to the data of Winson Green) are not available for other local prisons, or for training or central prisons; but it is possible to make some estimates of the kind of men these institutions contain, from knowledge of the total system's input and transfer policies. The data in these chapters relates mainly to 1967.

Chapter V deals with the question of changing the operation of the prison system, and with the effects on different parts of the system of changes in input (e.g. changes in sentencing policy). Important changes of this kind were made by the Criminal Justice Act 1967, some consequences of which are considered in this chapter. Finally, Chapter VI discusses possible future developments in the English prison system, with special reference to the policies set out in the recent White Paper *People in Prison.*[1] Some of the statistical tables in the book have been relegated to a Statistical Supplement, which appears after Chapter VI; references in the text to tables designated by the letter S followed by an Arabic number are references to tables in this Supplement. In some cases these tables are accompanied by additional comments, though these are not (I hope) necessary to the understanding of any point made in the text. Finally, in addition to the two appendices already mentioned (on mathematical models and the methodology of the Winson Green study) there is a short appendix on certain statistical methods used in this report, and one containing illustrative case histories of some of the 'long-term residents' of Winson Green prison.

[1] Henceforth cited simply as Cmnd. 4214.

II

The Structure and Input of the English Prison System

Types of prison in England

The institutions which comprise the English prison system can be classified into general local prisons; special local prisons; training prisons; central prisons; and remand centres.[1] With the exception of the general local prisons and remand centres, there are both open and closed institutions in each category. There are two institutions[2] entirely for male young prisoners, and one psychiatric prison[3]; and there are six prisons which contain women only.[4]

General local prisons are defined as prisons which receive prisoners under sentence direct from the courts. These institutions are thus the entry points for the prison system; all prisoners begin their sentences in general locals even if they are subsequently transferred to other types of institution. These prisons make up by far the largest sector of the system; as Table II.1 shows, in 1967 the 24 general local prisons held, between them, over half the average population of males in English prisons—that is, nearly four times as many as were serving sentences in open prisons. The general locals vary considerably in size; in 1967, about half had average populations of 300 or less, whereas the nine largest contained between three and four times

[1] This terminology, though not contained in the present Prison Rules (S.I. No. 388 of 1966), was still in use within the system at the end of 1969; it is convenient to use it to describe the structure of the system up to that time. Some changes in the system since then are mentioned in this chapter; others are discussed in Chapter V.

[2] Northallerton, in Yorkshire, and Aylesbury, in Buckinghamshire. In general, these institutions now take only young prisoners (i.e. those under 21 on reception) who are serving medium- and long-term sentences; those serving short sentences are usually retained in the general local prisons.

[3] Grendon Underwood, in Buckinghamshire.

[4] These six prisons, and their inmates, will not be considered in this book. There were only 2,051 females received into prison under sentence in 1967, and the average population serving sentences for criminal offences in that year was only 546. By 1969 these numbers had fallen to 1,422 and 464.

that number. These nine institutions—the four London prisons for males, and the general local prisons of Liverpool, Manchester, Leeds, Birmingham and Durham—together contained over a third of the English prison population in that year. But holding inmates under sentence is not the only function of the general locals. In addition, they contain unconvicted prisoners on remand awaiting

Table II.1

Institutional Capacity and Population in 1967 (Males only)

Type of Prison	*Capacity*	*Average Population*	*% of total Population*
General local prisons:			
4 London prisons*	3,538	4,728	17·6
5 Largest provincial prisons†	3,563	5,259	19·5
15 Other provincial prisons	3,520	4,792	17·8
Total (24)	10,621	14,779	54·9
Remand centres (9)	1,246	1,360	5·1
Special local prisons:			
Open (7)	2,716	2,513	9·3
Closed (4)	1,435	1,959	7·3
Total (11)	4,151	4,472	16·6
Training prisons:			
Open (3)	1,152	1,041	3·9
Closed (8)	2,632	2,092	7·8
Total (11)	3,784	3,133	11·6
Central prisons:			
Open (1)	432	391	1·5
Closed (5)	2,414	2,330	8·7
Total (6)	2,846	2,721	10·1
Other prisons‡ (3)	599	444	1·7
Total, all institutions (64)	23,247	26,909	100·0

* Brixton, Pentonville, Wandsworth, Wormwood Scrubs.
† Liverpool, Manchester, Birmingham, Leeds, Durham.
‡ Northallerton and Aylesbury young prisoners' centres and Grendon Underwood psychiatric prison (all closed).

trial, convicted prisoners who are on remand awaiting sentence and boys sentenced to borstal who are awaiting vacancies in the borstal allocation centres.[1] Prisoners on remand in fact made up over a fifth

[1] These centres, though strictly speaking part of the borstal system, are now located in Wormwood Scrubs and Manchester prisons. In 1967 it was not uncommon for boys to wait as long as four weeks in a general local prison before being transferred to an allocation centre. This poses a considerable problem in

of the population of the general local prisons in 1967.[1] One *remand centre* taking adult males was opened at Risley, in Lancashire, in 1965; this centre serves both the Liverpool and Manchester areas, so that the general locals in these cities no longer contain men on remand. In addition, there are now nine remand centres for males under 21 (including boys awaiting borstal allocation); some of these also contain female prisoners.

The other types of institution making up the English prison system —special local, training and central prisons—receive their inputs by transfer from the local prisons and they do not contain prisoners on remand. The method of allocation to these prisons was changed somewhat in 1967, after the system was divided for certain administrative purposes into four regions.[2] The broad principles, however, have so far apparently remained much the same as in earlier years.

Special local prisons—of which in 1967, seven were open institutions and four were closed—are basically 'satellites' of the general locals. They are intended to take short-term 'star' prisoners,[3] civil prisoners and others serving short sentences who cannot conveniently be kept in the general locals. Subject to rules restricting overcrowding in special locals, and the eligibility of certain types of offender for open prisons, allocation to special locals is primarily controlled by the staff of general local prisons; men are not selected for special locals on any kind of criteria of 'trainability', and in fact the receiving institutions have virtually no control over their inputs. This is the main feature distinguishing special local prisons from *training prisons* (formerly distinguished as *regional* training prisons and *corrective* training prisons), of which, in 1967, three were open prisons and eight closed. These institutions are intended for prisoners serving medium-term sentences (at present defined, generally speaking, as from one to three years for stars and one to five years for ordinaries).

---

many general locals, since these boys must, so far as is possible, be kept physically separate from adults under sentence. Though this problem has been eased somewhat by the opening of separate remand centres, the number of places in these centres has not kept up with the demand for them. See Cmnd. 4214, para 147; and below, pp. 100, 102.

[1] The composition of the average population of Winson Green prison in 1966, and of the sample described in the next chapter, are shown in Table B2 in Appendix B below, p. 127.

[2] See RPD (1967), p. 6, RPD (1965), p. 14; Cmnd. 4214, para 170; and cf. *The Sentence of the Court* (2nd ed. 1969), pp. 40–41.

[3] i.e. generally speaking those serving their first prison sentences. See p. 17 below.

Allocation to training prisons is more closely controlled by their own staffs; up to 1967, a usual practice was for the governor or an assistant governor from the training prison to meet with the staff of the general locals in his area to select men regarded as 'trainable', i.e. as suitable for allocation to the training prison. Training prisons thus draw their inmates from a number of local prisons, on the basis of criteria which—even if not uniform throughout the system—are nonetheless likely to result in a more homogeneous input than that of either general or special local prisons. Finally, *central prisons* are those taking prisoners serving long sentences; that is, at present, 'stars' serving over three years, and ordinary prisoners serving more than five years. Allocation to these six prisons—of which one is an open institution, the rest closed—was until 1967 done centrally, by the Prison Department of the Home Office. Since then, regional allocation centres have been set up in four general local prisons (Liverpool, Birmingham, Wandsworth and Bristol), to which long-term prisoners are sent for a period of assessment before being sent to a central prison.

It is important to note that the classification of institutions just described is to some extent a flexible one in practice; in recent years the functions and regimes of some institutions have been changed, in response to new training policies or changes in the input of the system. For example, the recent abolition of the special sentences of preventive detention and corrective training[1] has meant that prisons which formerly held only men serving these types of sentence have been given over to other uses; there has also been some transfer of institutions from the prison system to the borstal system (and vice versa) in recent years.[2] Moreover, while most English prisons can be classified as general or special local, training or central, according to their primary uses, some also have other and more specialized functions, or cater for special types of inmate. Thus, for example, there are hostels at a number of local prisons to which some long-term prisoners are returned near the end of their sentences; these prisoners work in the community for some months before being finally discharged. In 1967, there were special maximum-security wings at Durham, Leicester and Parkhurst prisons; treat-

[1] By the Criminal Justice Act 1967, s. 37; see below, pp. 72–74.

[2] Thus, for example, in 1966 Stoke Heath, a closed training prison, was converted to a borstal because of heavy pressure on accommodation in closed borstals: see RPD (1966), p. 8; and the recall borstals at Reading and Portsmouth have more recently been reconverted to prisons. See RPD (1968), p. 3.

ment units for alcoholics at Wakefield (a central prison), Spr
(a special local) and Pentonville (a general local); and Stafford
(a closed special local) contained young prisoners as well as s
term and medium-term stars who were considered unsuitable
open conditions. There are indications that this mixing of functions may increase in the future.[1] Nonetheless, broadly speaking, the structure of the system is still as I have just described it.

Regimes and conditions

Table II.2 shows that at the end of 1967, the average male population of the English prison system as a whole exceeded the system's total capacity by about 15 per cent. The table also reveals that this over-

Table II.2

Capacity and Population of English prisons for males: 1956 and 1967

	Type of Institution				
	General Local	*Remand Centres*	*Open*	*Other Closed*	*Total*
1956:					
Capacity	10,041	—	2,041	6,075	18,157
Average population	10,718	—	1,569	4,916	17,203
% of capacity	*106·7*	—	*76·9*	*80·9*	*94·7*
1967:					
Capacity	10,621	1,246	4,300	7,080	23,247
Average population	14,779	1,360	3,945	6,825	26,909
% of capacity	*139·1*	*109·1*	*91·7*	*96·4*	*115·8*

Source: RPD (1956), RPD (1967).

crowding of the whole system took place entirely in the preceding decade. At the end of 1956, the male population of the system was roughly what it had been at the end of the war. Annual receptions of males under sentence were at their lowest level since 1940, and few institutions were overcrowded; the system as a whole was only about nine-tenths full. But by 1967, the average population of male

[1] See Cmnd. 4214, paras 190–191; and below, pp. 94–95. It should also be noted that the classification system described here only applies to institutions for males. Brief functional descriptions of the English prisons are given in the Prison Department's annual reports; see, e.g. RPD (1968), pp. 34–39; and Cmnd. 4214, pp. 82–85.

prisoners had grown by about 75 per cent, and in the system as a whole there were about six men for every five places.[1] As the table also shows, this overcrowding was entirely confined to the general local prisons. The numbers in other types of institution have not been allowed to exceed capacity; the result is that the average population of the general locals rose by about half in the years 1956–67, though their total capacity increased by only a fifth in that time. As a result, by the end of 1967, nearly half of the men in these prisons were sleeping three in a cell.[2] In fact, in some of the smaller local prisons the situation must have been even worse. In Canterbury prison, for example, which has a cellular capacity of 159, the population in 1966 was 351 on average, and 403 at its highest—221 per cent and 253 per cent, respectively, of capacity.

The extreme overcrowding in the general local prisons places severe limitations on the regimes of these institutions. In most training and central prisons, it is now possible for inmates to work a reasonably full week; one training new prison—Coldingley, in Surrey—is designed as an 'industrial prison', in which 80 per cent of the inmates will be employed on light engineering and other industrial work which is intended to be competitive with outside industry.[3] In most general locals, however, the inmates now work no more than sixteen hours a week; in many cases the time which the prisoners actually spend at work is much less than this.[4] The poor physical condition of the general local prisons is well-known; all of them are at least a century old, and many have insufficient space for workshops or recreational activities. Some attempts have been made in recent years to overcome the limitations of these prisons;

[1] For a summary of trends in crime in England and Wales in this period, and of the sentencing practices of the courts in relation to imprisonment, see Cmnd. 4214, pp. 10–19. It is important to note (a) that the main factor responsible for the increase in receptions into prison in 1956–67 has been the increase in persons convicted during that period, and that the proportion of convicted offenders sent to prison has in fact slightly declined; (b) that though the *average* length of sentence has increased over this period by nearly 20 per cent, this is largely due to a reduction in the number of very short prison sentences, and does not indicate a general increase in the severity of prison sentences passed by the courts (for comparable types of crime) over this period. See further below, pp. 56–61.

[2] According to RPD (1967), p. 1, the total number of men sleeping three in a cell at the end of 1967 was 6,342; virtually all of these men must have been in local prisons.

[3] See Cmnd. 4214, paras 50–56; and for an earlier study of work in a typical training prison (Maidstone) see M. H. Cooper and R. D. King, 'Social and Economic Problems of Prisoners' Work', in P. Halmos (ed) *Sociological Review Monograph*, No. 9 (1965), pp. 145–174.

[4] Cf. RPD (1964), p. 46; and see T. and P. Morris, *Pentonville* (London: Routledge, 1963), pp. 28–29.

the so-called 'Norwich system', providing for increased association between inmates and contact with staff, was introduced in a number of other local prisons in the late 1950's. But the operation of this scheme is now very limited by overcrowding, in most of these prisons.[1] For example, at the time of our survey at Winson Green prison in 1966, there were probably over 100 men in the prison who were technically eligible to dine 'in association'; but less than 40 were actually able to do so, owing to shortage of space and staff.

The general local prisons are further hampered, in dealing with men under sentence, by the fact that—in the words of the recent White Paper—'the first responsibility of any local prison is to the courts. The first priority in the deployment of its staff is in the reception of prisoners from court and despatch to court, in escorting prisoners to and from the higher courts and in ensuring their security'.[2] Escort duty makes heavy demands on the prison staff. Winson Green, for example, in 1966 held prisoners on remand from a total of 41 magistrates' courts, eleven courts of quarter sessions and three assizes, located in three large counties. During most of 1966, there were between 80 and 90 basic-grade prison officers on duty in Winson Green; but on most weekdays when the courts were sitting, at least a quarter of these officers would be away from the prison, escorting prisoners to the courts. On a number of occasions, during assizes and quarter sessions, the number of officers actually in the prison fell to less than 50. At these times, there was no alternative but to close the prison's workshops and confine the men in their cells. With luck, part of one shop in which star prisoners worked could be kept open; otherwise, apart from two half-hour exercise periods, the men were kept 'banged up' in their cells the whole day.[3]

[1] For a study of the effects of introducing the so-called 'Norwich system' into Bristol prison, see now F. E. Emery, *Freedom and Justice within Walls* (London: Tavistock, 1970). The research on which this book is based, however, was carried out in the years 1957–60, when the average population of Bristol prison was 366; in 1967 it was 510.

[2] Cmnd. 4214, p. 67.

[3] There is an extra irony in this. Just over half of our sample of 167 prisoners were kept three in a cell throughout their sentences; another 10 per cent were 'three'd up' for more than half of the time they were in Winson Green. But the remaining men spent most of their time in single cells, and nearly a quarter of the men were never kept three in a cell during the time they were in the local prison. Understandably, it was the policy of the staff to provide men serving longer sentences with single cells wherever possible. But this humane policy, coupled with the limitations imposed by escort duties, had the consequence that prisoners serving longer sentences were subjected to periods of virtual solitary confinement —a regime somewhat more repressive than the 'separate system' for which Winson Green was originally built.

The regimes of closed prisons in England were further affected by the implementation, in 1967, of the security precautions recommended by the Mountbatten Report.[1] In its annual report for 1968 the Prison Department referred to 'gloomy predictions at the time of the Mountbatten Report that the increased emphasis on security would seriously affect the development of liberal regimes in closed prisons', adding that 'these have not been fulfilled'.[2] Yet in its report for 1967, the Department had stated that 'Preoccupation with [security] measures inevitably had a profound effect on the working of prison service establishments. Staff who had long been encouraged to develop treatment relationships toward prisoners had little time left for this important work after discharging tasks arising from the need to concentrate on security. . . .'[3] The prisons said to have been the most affected were the large closed prisons such as Wormwood Scrubs and Wakefield, which had developed 'training regimes'. It has been suggested[4] that there was something of a panic reaction among prison staff, following the Mountbatten Report; this is certainly consistent with my own observations during this period at Winson Green prison, where the long-sentence men in the prison were suddenly stopped from dining in association. These initial extreme reactions appeared to have been relaxed somewhat after a few months, so far as dining out, classes and the like were concerned; and this no doubt happened at other prisons as well. However, as already noted, the regimes of the general local prisons were unavoid-

[1] The Report on Prison Escapes and Security (Lord Mountbatten's Report), Cmnd. 3175 of 1966.

[2] See RPD (1968), p. 5. The report adds that 'When the position was reviewed in autumn 1968 it was found that in the great majority of prisons the educational and other activities had either been unaffected by the Mountbatten Report or had since been restored to normal. The small number of prisons which had not been able to resume all their former activities, for example outside activities, were still able to pursue a satisfactory programme.'

[3] See RPD (1967), p. 5. The 'adjustments' in the regimes of these prisons are described by an extract from a report made by the Governor of Wakefield, which states, *inter alia*, that 'at the beginning of the year it was noticeable that the hitherto excellent staff/inmate relationship had suffered a severe setback and officers felt, with some justification, that everything must be sacrificed to security. However, with a larger staff and consequently more continuity on the wings, a much better atmosphere is developing, and we are slowly but surely returning to the more normal relationships which have existed for so long at Wakefield.'

[4] By Mr H. J. Klare, Secretary of the Howard League, in evidence to the Sub-Committee on Social Affairs of the Estimates Committee: see the Minutes of Evidence accompanying the Committee's Eleventh Report (H.C.599 of 1967), at p. 290. On the costs of the Mountbatten recommendations, estimated at £2½ million in 1967–68, see the same Committee's Report, paras 37–42.

ably extremely restrictive, even before the implementation of the Mountbatten Committee's recommendations.

Some further important differences between institutions of different types will emerge in later chapters, when we consider the inputs and populations of those institutions. First, however, we must describe the allocation policies and other factors which govern transfers between the different sectors of the prison system.

Inter-institutional relationships

As we have already noted, the general local prisons are the entry points for the English prison system; consequently, they are mainly 'exporting' prisons in relation to the rest of the system. Unfortunately, allocation policies and practices governing transfers within the system have not yet been the subject of empirical research; and there are no published statistics on the flows of prisoners between institutions of different types.[1] However, it is possible to identify some of the main factors which influence these flows.

Some of the primary criteria governing transfers to special local, training, and central prisons have already been mentioned in passing. One is the inmate's previous criminality and/or previous prison experience. As is well-known, prisoners in the English system are classified administratively into 'stars' and 'ordinaries'—star prisoners being, in general, those who are serving their first sentences, and ordinaries being those who have been 'inside' before.[2] The distinction between these two groups is not, in practice, an absolute one; an ordinary may be upgraded to star status at the discretion of the prison Governor and a star may be reclassified as an ordinary if he absconds or otherwise misbehaves during his sentence. Thus there is a certain overlap between the two groups in terms of their previous prison experience. There is an even greater overlap in terms of previous criminality, since star prisoners are by no means all first offenders; indeed, the majority of stars have one or more previous

[1] The Home Office is developing a computerized index of prisoners, which should in future provide more information, for both administrative and research purposes, about the movements of prisoners within the system. Ideally, however, this information should be supplemented by research on the decision-making process itself. For a discussion of borstal allocation see R. L. Morrison, 'Borstal Allocation' (1957), 8 *Brit. J. Delinq.* 95.

[2] These terms, formerly defined by statutory instrument, are not used in the latest Prison Rules (S.I. No. 388 of 1964). But they are still in general use within the system, with the meanings indicated in the text.

proved offences on their first arrival in prison.[1] Still, the distinction between the two groups is intended to reflect, and does reflect, a broad difference in their previous criminality (or 'criminal sophistication'); and in general the two groups are kept apart within the system, no doubt on the basis of the time-honoured dogma that inmates who are more criminal are likely to 'contaminate' those who are less so.[2]

A second factor governing allocation—and probably one of even greater importance than previous criminality—is the prisoner's length of sentence. In general, men serving short sentences—of, say, a year or less—are kept in general local or special local prisons. Men serving medium-length sentences—of one year up to three in the case of stars, and one year up to five in the case of ordinaries—may be transferred to training prisons; stars serving over three years, and ordinaries serving over five years, are sent to central prisons. In practice, the cutting points between 'long', 'medium' and 'short' sentences are not invariable: a prisoner serving a fairly long sentence may be sent to a training prison (or even retained in a general local prison) if there are special reasons for doing this, e.g. a need for special medical treatment or his family situation. Moreover, the transfer from general locals of all types of prisoner is subject to an important constraint, namely the limited capacity of special local, training and central prisons: these institutions are not allowed to become overcrowded, and in fact most have been less than full in recent years.

A third factor, of increasing importance since the implementation of the Mountbatten Report's recommendations, is the apparent risk that the prisoner will escape. Prisoners are now placed in one of the following four security categories:[3]

[1] Thus a recent survey of married prisoners found that 18·6 per cent of those classified as stars had in fact served at least one previous sentence, whereas 13 per cent of the ordinaries were only serving their second sentence: see P. Morris, *Prisoners and their Families* (London: Routledge, 1965), pp. 53–54. For a similar finding see T. and P. Morris, *Pentonville*, pp. 52–53.

[2] Certain other groups must, so far as is possible, be kept segregated from adult prisoners under sentence: these include *young prisoners* (those under 21); *civil prisoners* (those committed for non-payment of debts, maintenance to wives, or contempt of court); *unconvicted prisoners* (who are awaiting trial); and *unsentenced prisoners* (who have been remanded after conviction, to await sentence). Until 1968, certain persistent offenders were classified as *corrective trainees* and *preventive detainees*; these special forms of sentence are now abolished, though the latter has been replaced by a similar measure, the 'extended sentence' (Criminal Justice Act 1967, s. 38).

[3] See Cmnd. 3175, paras 212, 217.

Category A. Prisoners whose escape would be highly dangerous to the public or the police, or to the security of the state.

Category B. Prisoners for whom the very highest conditions of security are not necessary, but for whom escape must be made very difficult.

Category C. Prisoners who cannot be trusted in open conditions, but who do not have the ability or resources to make a determined escape attempt.

Category D. Those who can reasonably be trusted to serve their sentences in open conditions.

It is now officially estimated that about one per cent of all convicted prisoners in custody will be in Category A, about 30 per cent in Category B, about 50 per cent in Category C and 20 per cent in Category D.[1] Allocation to open prisons, however, is limited by another factor in addition to the likelihood of escape. In general, prisoners convicted of sexual offences or violence against the person, or who have in the past been convicted of such offences, are not sent to open institutions.[2]

Fourthly, allocation to training prisons is governed to some extent by a concept of 'trainability'—that is, amenability to, or likelihood of benefiting from, the regime of a training prison. This concept is in practice a vague one; its use appears to vary considerably, both in different institutions and from one time to another. But it seems to be related largely to a lack of previous criminality and/or previous prison experience, though other things such as the prisoner's work skills and work experience are no doubt also considered.[3]

In addition to the transfer of inmates from the general local prisons to other sectors of the system, there is some movement of prisoners from one general local to another, chiefly because of overcrowding. Moreover, a proportion of those transferred to other types of prison are subsequently transferred back to general locals, for a

[1] Cmnd. 4214, p. 69.

[2] Ibid. A few prisoners serving long sentences for sexual or violent crimes are transferred, toward the end of their sentences, to Leyhill open prison; but where other open prisons are concerned, the Prison Department must observe undertakings given when the prisons are opened, that inmates convicted of offences involving sex or violence will not be sent there.

[3] This at least is the impression which we gained from conversations with governors, assistant governors and other prison staff during our research in 1966 and 1967. The classification of certain ordinaries as 'trainable' also appears to be influenced, however, by the number of available vacancies in training prisons. See below, pp. 51–52.

variety of reasons. Some are found to be unsuitable for training prisons; some are to be produced in court, either as witnesses or to face further charges; some are nearing the end of long sentences mostly spent in central prisons, or are having 'accumulated visits' from wives or families. Thus, for example, of the 6,723 receptions into Winson Green in 1966, 6 per cent were transferred in—though the majority of these men had begun their sentences in Winson Green in earlier years.[1]

Relations between imprisonment and other penal measures

The connections between the prison system and the rest of the penal system can be studied in two ways. The first is by research on decision-making by the courts (and, at an earlier stage, the police);[2] the second is by comparison of the characteristics of offenders sent to prison with those of offenders dealt with in other ways. Much more research of each kind is needed; the first kind, in particular, has been very much neglected. Research on the use by the British police of their discretion not to prosecute offenders is virtually non-existent;[3] and most of the research done to date on the sentencing practices of the courts has been concerned with the problem of disparity in sentencing—that is, with investigating differences between sentencers in the ways in which they deal with similar types of offender.[4] Though it is undoubtedly true that some such differences do exist, in particular at magistrates' courts, concentration on these differences may have led researchers to neglect somewhat the extent to which the policies of different sentencers are similar, and the

[1] See Table B.1. p. 125

[2] A similar decision-making process goes on at a still earlier stage, of course: victims (and others who believe offences to have been committed by a known person) must decide whether to report the suspected offender to the police. But while these decisions to some extent control the input to the penal system, they are not made by agents of the system: I shall therefore not consider them.

[3] American studies of this process include I. Piliavin and S. Briar, 'Police Encou nterswith Juveniles', (1964) 70 *Am. J. Sociol.*, 206–214; Jerome Skolnick, *Justice Without Trial* (New York: Wiley 1964), esp. pp. 80 ff; C. Werthman and I. Piliavin, 'Gang Members and the, Police', in D. Bordua (ed), *The Police: Six Sociological Essays* (New York: Wiley, 1964), pp. 72 ff; A. Cicourel, *The Social Organization of Juvenile Justice* (New York: Wiley, 1968); R. M. Terry, 'Discrimination in the handling of juvenile offenders by social-control agencies', (1967) *J. Res. Crime & Delinq.*, 218.

[4] See, for example, Roger Hood, *Sentencing in Magistrates' Courts* (London: Stevens, 1962); E. Green, *Judicial Attitudes in Sentencing* (London: Macmillan, 1961).

extent to which the sentencing practices of the courts as a whole are both stable and consistent, at least in the short run.

A court's choice of sentence may of course legitimately be based on a large number of different factors, depending on the type of case; and it may further be influenced by such things as the court's perception of the facts concerning the offence or the offender, or the inadequacy of facilities for certain types of treatment (for example, a shortage of places in institutions or probation case-loads). It seems clear that in general, however, the sentences imposed by the English courts (at least on adult offenders) are very largely determined by relatively few factors, of which the perceived gravity of the offender's crime and the number of times he has previously been convicted are especially important. As we shall see,[1] the first of these things strongly influences the length of the prison sentences imposed by the courts. For our present purposes, however, it is the second factor—previous convictions—which is relevant, since it largely determines the connections which exist, in practice, between different parts of the penal system.

For the majority of adult offenders, both magistrates' courts and higher courts had, before 1968, a choice between four different types of penal measure: the fine, discharge (either absolute or conditional), probation and imprisonment. The evidence from a number of studies shows that for those who have not previously been convicted, the courts tended, *ceteris paribus*, to use four measures in the order of frequency just mentioned: the majority being fined or discharged, and only a small proportion being imprisoned. For recidivists, the order of frequency is reversed: as the number of previous convictions increases, the probability of receiving a sentence of imprisonment increases and the probability of either a fine or discharge correspondingly falls. Thus, in Dr W. H. Hammond's sample of 2,198 adult offenders convicted in the Metropolitan Police District in 1957, about one-third were first offenders: of these, 50 per cent were fined, 23 per cent were discharged and only 14 per cent imprisoned. Of those in this sample with one or more previous convictions, 54 per cent were imprisoned, whereas only 22 per cent were fined and 11 per cent discharged.[2] Further analysis of some of Hammond's data, as it is reported by Walker,[3] shows that for male offenders aged 21–29

[1] See below, pp. 60–61.
[2] See *The Sentence of the Court* (2nd ed. 1969), pp. 67, 69.
[3] N. Walker, *Sentencing in a Rational Society* (London: Allen Lane, 1969), p. 204.

the probability of imprisonment rises sharply with the number of previous convictions: it is ·141 for first offenders, and ·581 for those making their fourth court appearance. At the same time, the probability of receiving a fine drops from ·489 to ·189, and that of being discharged falls from ·195 to ·041. A similar finding, so far as the use of imprisonment is concerned, emerged from Hood's study of sentences imposed by twelve English magistrates' courts on adult males convicted of indictable offences. Of those with no previous convictions of this type, 9 per cent were imprisoned; of those with five or more previous convictions, 77 per cent were imprisoned.[1] Exactly the same pattern is observed in the careers of 157 recidivists in the Winson Green prison population sample to be described in the next chapter. The probability of being sent to prison rises steadily, from about ·075 on the first court appearance to ·575 on the tenth.

The probability of being placed on probation remained relatively constant, in the Hammond-Walker data, at about one in five for each of the first four court appearances. It is possible that some courts tend to use probation for adult second offenders who were fined or discharged on their first appearance in court, before proceeding to imprisonment. But the available evidence suggests that in general there is a greater tendency for courts to use probation for those recidivists who have previously been on probation, and similarly to stick to fines and discharges for recidivists who have not had probation. This probably reflects the influence of probation officers' views (as expressed in social enquiry reports) on selection for probation: those thought unsuitable on their first court appearance are also likely to be unsuitable on subsequent court appearances.[2] The result seems to be that the fine (or discharge) and probation are generally separate routes to imprisonment, rather than being successive steps along the same route.

The probabilities just quoted refer to the sentences imposed by the courts on convicted offenders; they take no account of cautioning

[1] Roger Hood, *op. cit.*, p. 137. For a similar finding in an American jurisdiction (Philadelphia) see Edward Green, *op. cit.*, pp. 43, 44, 114–115.

[2] For evidence on the influence of social enquiry reports on selection for probation in England see F. V. Jarvis, 'Inquiry before sentence', in T. Grygier *et al* (eds), *Criminology in Transition* (London: Tavistock, 1965) 43, at 60; for an American study with a similar finding see R. M. Carter and L. T. Wilkins, 'Some Factors in Sentencing Policy' (1967) 58, *J. Crim. L., Crim. & P.S.*, 503–514. On the tendency of English courts to use probation for first offenders, L. Radzinowicz (ed), *The Results of Probation* (London: Macmillan, 1958), pp. 14, 65; M. Davies, *Probationers in their Social Environment* (London: HMSO, 1969), p. 18.

by the police, or of offenders who are acquitted. In addition, they take no account of the fact that a small proportion of those offenders who are fined by the courts are subsequently committed to prison (usually for a short term) for non-payment of the fines. As we shall see, because the number of offenders fined is so large, these 'fine-defaulters' form a fairly large fraction of all receptions into prison under sentence in any year. For the moment, however, the important point is that imprisonment without the option of a fine tends to be reserved by the courts for those offenders (mostly males over 21) who have demonstrably failed to be reformed (or deterred from further crime) by other penal measures. In 1967, as Table S.1 shows, only 8 per cent of adult males received into prison were first offenders; about two-thirds had five or more previous proved offences. About three-fourths had been to prison (or some other penal institution) at least once; a quarter had had five or more previous institutional sentences.

No doubt this policy is due to economic considerations in the minds of sentencers, as well as to the notion of a 'tariff' based in part on recidivism.[1] There is a further factor to be taken into consideration, however, in assessing the operation of the penal system. This is that the greater the number of an offender's previous convictions, the greater the probability that he will be reconvicted. There are, of course, other factors which have generally been found to be associated with reconvictions: age at first conviction, time since last conviction, and type of offence are among the most important of these.[2] Contrariwise, there is a negative association between age and likelihood of reconviction: other things being equal, the older an offender is at the time of his appearance in court, the less likely he is to appear there again. But for any age-group, and particularly for adult offenders, the number of previous convictions is probably the strongest single predictor of recidivism. The more often one has been through the penal system, the more likely one is to return to it.[3] Those committed to prison have in general been through the

[1] Again, though empirical evidence from Britain is not available, it is likely that similar considerations weigh with the police in the decision to caution rather than prosecute.

[2] For evidence on some of these factors, see T. Sellin, 'Recidivism and Maturation', (1958) *Nat. Prob. and Parole Assoc. J.*, p. 241; D. Glaser, *The Effectiveness of a Prison and Parole System* (Indianapolis: Bobbs Merrill, 1964), Chap. 3; W. H. Hammond and E. Chayen, *Persistent Criminals* (London: HMSO, 1963) pp. 101–107, 153–164; H. Mannheim and L. T. Wilkins, *Prediction Methods in Relation to Borstal Training* (London: HMSO, 1955).

[3] See *The Sentence of the Court*, *op. cit.*, pp. 64–66.

system most often; they are therefore most likely to return to it, quite apart from any question of the 'effectiveness' of the prison system itself.

The combination of these two things gives rise to something like the following, in terms of the movement of offenders through the penal system. Of all offenders who become known to the police in any year, the majority have not previously been apprehended. The bulk of these first offenders are either cautioned, or, if taken to court, are fined, discharged or placed on probation; the majority of them are not reconvicted. Of those who are convicted a second time, fewer are cautioned, fined or discharged, and a greater proportion are imprisoned; a higher proportion are convicted again; and so on. Another way to look at this matter is to consider a birth cohort of the male population over its life span. Members of this cohort begin to enter the English penal system at the age of ten;[1] the greatest number enter at about the age of fourteen, though a third or more do not enter for the first time until after the age of 21. Over the lifetime of such a cohort, it has been estimated that no fewer than 29 per cent will be convicted at least once of an indictable offence.[2] Those apprehended more than once will tend, with increasing probability, to enter institutions such as approved schools, detention centres, borstals and prisons; and of those passing through institutions for young offenders a substantial fraction will go to prison one or more times, later in life. Those passing through the system repeatedly will have, as we have noted, an increasing tendency to return to it; but there will naturally be new first entrants from the cohort throughout its life, and at each stage some of those who pass through the penal system will not re-enter it, either because they have in some sense been 'reformed' or because they have died or otherwise been removed from risk. Of course in any one year most sectors of the penal system will have inputs drawn not just from one such cohort, but from many.

[1] But see now the Children and Young Persons Act 1969, s. 4 (which when implemented will prohibit criminal proceedings, except for murder, in respect of acts done by persons under the age of fourteen).

[2] See the estimates by G. N. G. Rose and N. H. Avison, in L. Radzinowicz, *Ideology and Crime* (London: Heinemann, 1966) pp. 129–132. For a similar estimate of the risk of arrest for non-traffic offences, see R. Christensen, 'Projected Percentage of U.S. Population with Criminal Arrest and Conviction Records', Appendix J in President's Commission on Law Enforcement and Administration of Justice, Task Force Report on Science and Technology (1967), pp. 216–228, esp. 222.

At this point a *caveat* is necessary. The classification of English prisons as general local, special local, training and central (and the subdivision of the last three groups into open and closed institutions) certainly reflects real differences between those prisons, in terms of the numbers and types of inmates with which they deal; it also reflects some real differences between the regimes and conditions of the institutions. At the same time, there may well be important differences in these or other respects, between the prisons *within* any of those groups: the various sectors of the system are not necessarily entirely homogeneous. For example, the input of each general local prison depends on the pattern of crime in that prison's area, and the sentencing practices of the courts which it serves; and transfers from the prison will depend, *inter alia*, on the amount of prison accommodation of different types which is available. Since there are (or may be) regional variations in these factors, there are likely to be some differences between the populations of the general local prisons. For example, those located in large urban areas, with higher crime rates and (probably) larger recidivist populations, might be expected to have fewer 'star' prisoners among their inputs than the smaller prisons in more rural areas. Unfortunately, there are insufficient data available at present to allow these differences to be studied.

Nonetheless, the existence of such differences does not mean that it is useless to study the interrelationships between the different sectors of the prison system, and the movement of convicted offenders through that system; nor does it mean that the prisons as a group cannot usefully be regarded as one sector of the larger penal system, and studied in the same way. We shall see in the next chapter that the input of Winson Green (Birmingham) prison in 1966, though differing to some extent in composition from the total input of the system in 1966 and 1967, was by no means unrepresentative of it; my own opinion is that in 1966 Winson Green was very similar, in both regime and population, to the other large urban local prisons,[1] and that it was not in any sense specially *un*typical of the 24 general

[1] i.e. Liverpool, Manchester, Leeds and Durham. There are some differences between these institutions and the four London prisons for males—Brixton, Wandsworth, Pentonville and Wormwood Scrubs—though in terms of input and population these may largely disappear if the London prisons are considered together. The regimes of Liverpool and Manchester were changed to some extent by the opening of Risley Remand Centre in 1965, and the consequent removal of prisoners on remand from those institutions. See RPD (1965), p. 1; RPD (1964), p. 58.

locals as a group. Moreover, despite recent developments, there is still every reason to believe that the population of Winson Green is still fairly similar, in all relevant respects, to what it was in 1966. The picture presented in the next chapter may now be inaccurate in matters of detail; but it is still a pretty good likeness.

III

The Input and Population of Local Prisons

Receptions under sentence

In 1967, the total number of receptions of adult males into prison in England, under sentence for criminal offences, was 42,674. Of this total, 11,109—or over one-quarter—were receptions in default of the payment of a fine.[1] Since all of these receptions were initially into general local prisons, the input of this group of institutions can be described, in broad terms, from the statistics published annually by the Prison Department of the Home Office.[2] These statistics for the year 1967 are summarized in Table S.1. It will be seen from this table that in that year about one-quarter of receptions under sentence without the option of a fine were of men under sentence for breaking offences, with offenders convicted of simple and minor forms of larceny accounting for a slightly smaller fraction. Of those imprisoned for non-payment of fines, about one-third had been convicted of drunkenness; another third had been convicted of

[1] It is important to note that these figures are of receptions under sentence, and not of different persons: a small proportion of men are received into prison twice in the year, and are thus counted twice in the statistics. In our Winson Green sample, the figure was about 1 per cent; but this may well understate the size of the 'stage army' of drunks, vagrants, etc., who enter local prisons—especially in the big cities—more than once a year. It should also be noted that in 1967 there were 3,493 receptions of young prisoners under sentence (including fine-defaulters); in addition, 10 men were received under sentences of corrective training, and six under extended sentences.

[2] The Department's statistics use the term 'previous proved offences'; however, when an offender is dealt with at the same time for more than one offence, only one offence is recorded (this offence—the 'principal current offence'—is the one for which the longest sentence is imposed; if concurrent sentences of equal length are imposed, it is the one carrying the longest maximum sentence). Thus the Prison Department's statistics actually give the number of previous occasions on which the offender has been convicted, or previous court appearances (ignoring those leading to acquittal). This must be distinguished from the total number of offences of which the offender has been convicted at his previous court appearances; as we shall see (below, pp. 37–38), the two are quite different for many prisoners.

indictable offences, of which simple and minor larcenies accounted for about half.

As has already been noted, the great majority of these men are recidivists when they enter prison. Less than 8 per cent of the 'no option' receptions had not previously been convicted, and about two-thirds had been convicted five or more times; among the fine-defaulters the comparable figures are 12 per cent and 61 per cent. Only about a quarter of the 'no option' group had served no previous sentences in penal institutions, and a similar proportion had served five or more; among the fine-defaulters 45 per cent were serving their first institutional sentences. The bulk of these men's sentences on reception are short: 60 per cent of the 'no option' prisoners received in 1967 were serving six months or less, whereas 96 per cent of the fine-defaulters were under sentence of three months or less. But there are, of course, wide variations in length of sentence among those convicted of different offences: in particular, those imprisoned for crimes of violence (including robbery) and for sexual offences tend to be serving longer sentences than those convicted of property crimes.

A similar picture emerges from the more detailed data which we collected for a 10 per cent sample of receptions into Winson Green in 1966.[1] After deducting men on remand only, men transferred in, young prisoners and civil prisoners, this sample contained 374 receptions: of these 260, or 70 per cent, were imprisoned without the option of a fine, and the remaining 114 were fine-defaulters. There were some differences in respect of current offence, length of sentence, etc., between this sample and all receptions of adult men under sentence in 1966; in particular, offenders convicted of drunkenness accounted for almost half of the fine-defaulters, against about one-third for the country as a whole. This difference in the penological problem of drunkenness is probably to be expected, however, in a large urban area (especially one containing a relatively large Irish population, as Birmingham does); and in other respects our sample is reasonably representative of the input to general local prisons in recent years, up to 1967. Both 'no option' prisoners and fine-defaulters, of course, contribute to the population of the prison system. But they do so in very different proportions; and since they differ in a number of other respects, they must be considered separately.

[1] Details of the sampling method are given in Appendix B, p. 125.

Information on the previous convictions and previous penal experience of our sample could be obtained—from the prison, the Criminal Record Office at Scotland Yard and the Birmingham city police—for 231 of the 'no option' men and 100 of the fine-defaulters. These data are rather uneven, in addition to being incomplete; and in all probability they give a more favourable picture of the men's previous recorded criminality (especially for those serving very short sentences) than would be revealed by more complete information. The mean number of previous court appearances among the 231 'no option' men was 7·2; if we consider only those occasions on which the men were convicted of indictable offences, however, the mean is 5·2, and the median is slightly lower. Those whose 1966 sentence was for a property offence had significantly worse records than those convicted of violence, robbery and sexual offences. This is not to say that the latter group were largely first or 'accidental' offenders. On the contrary, they had on average been convicted on 2·75 occasions for indictable offences, and 5·8 occasions for offences of all kinds. But since a lengthy criminal record and a record of violent or sexual crime now both tend, independently, to reduce the probability of transfer to an open prison, it is important to note that these things are themselves to some degree negatively associated, affecting different groups of men received into the prison system.[1]

As would be expected, a substantial fraction of the men had been convicted as juveniles: nearly a quarter had appeared in court before the age of 14. Of those with convictions as juveniles, about 30 per cent had been committed to an approved school, detention centre or borstal on one occasion, and a slightly larger proportion had been in more than one of these institutions. It is of interest to note, however, that on the available evidence, over a third of the 'no option' receptions had not been convicted before the age of 21. Some allowance must be made for the imperfections of official criminal records in the 1940's, when most of these men were juveniles. Even so, the sample appears to contain a relatively large group of 'latecomers' to crime. These men had significantly less previous imprisonment than those with convictions as juveniles; nonetheless,

[1] See below, pp. 50–52. Another factor which is relevant for this purpose is a history of *previous* violent or sexual crime. But of the 160 'no option' men in our sample serving sentences for property crimes, over 10 per cent had been convicted on at least one previous occasion of an offence of violence; a further 5 per cent had been convicted of a sexual offence; and two men had been convicted of both violent and sexual offences.

about half of them had been imprisoned without the option of a fine on one or more previous occasions. In view of the extensive criminal records of the 'no option' group, it is perhaps surprising that 44 per cent of those whose records we could trace had not been on probation.

The fine-defaulters for whom previous criminal records could be obtained had, on average, been convicted on 9·7 previous occasions; if indictable offences only are considered, the average is 3·2. But these figures misrepresent, to some extent, the nature of the previous criminality of this group; in particular, though the men convicted of drunkenness tended to have very long records of previous court appearances, most of them had seldom been convicted of any other type of crime. Our data undoubtedly understate the previous prison experience of this group, since imprisonment for non-payment of fines is very seldom revealed by official criminal records. Half of these men had not been previously imprisoned without the option of a fine, and only 10 per cent had five or more such sentences; only a quarter had been convicted as juveniles, and a similar proportion had previously been on probation. However, if the men convicted of drunkenness are excluded, the remainder have criminal and penal records which are not dissimilar to those of men imprisoned without the option of a fine; they have far more previous criminality than the typical adult male offender who is fined by the English courts.[1]

Another point which emerges from our data on the Winson Green receptions is that in addition to their principal offences, the men in our sample had been dealt with for a large number of other offences: prison, it seems, is a place where a good deal of crime catches up with those who are sent there. Over half of the whole sample had been convicted of one or more additional offences and about 8 per cent had offences taken into consideration by the courts in sentencing; 22 men had warrants lodged at the prison during their sentences, in respect of unpaid fines.[2] In addition, after having been received

[1] In the sample of 690 offenders over 21 included in the Home Office study *The Sentence of the Court*, who had been fined, 375 or 54·4 per cent were apparently first offenders; this compared with 7 out of 53 (i.e. 13·2 per cent) in our sample, and 13 per cent among all fine-defaulters imprisoned in 1966, according to the Prison Department's statistics.

[2] This is often done at the offender's request; understandably so, since in most cases the time in default is served concurrently with the sentence which the man is already serving. About three-quarters of those with additional offences also received concurrent sentences for those offences rather than consecutive ones. This is the policy which is usually to be followed by the courts in cases where the additional offences are committed on the same occasion as the principal offence,

into prison under sentence (and thus entered in the Prison Department's statistics of receptions), 26 of the men in the sample—that is, 7 per cent—were produced in court again, convicted of further offences, and given additional sentences. In many cases, such sentences 'on production' extend the effective lengths of the men's sentences by a considerable amount, though this is not revealed by the published statistics, which now take no account of productions at all. This point is especially important in relation to fine-defaulters, of whom (if our sample is representative) about one in nine is produced again in court. Not all of those produced in this way were given prison sentences on their second appearances in court; and some who were, received fairly short or concurrent terms which did not add much to the time they spent in prison. But for some of this group (especially among the fine-defaulters), the effective length of sentence was substantially increased; no less than half of the sentences imposed on production were for over one year.[1]

The average time from first reception under sentence to production was just over a month for the 'no option' men, and two weeks for fine-defaulters. But a few waited as long as three months before returning to court. For this reason, and because of the small numbers in our sample, it is not easy to estimate the amount which production tends to add to the length of sentences originally received. Even if productions are taken into account, however, the great majority of men received into prison in England are committed there for relatively short periods of time, bearing in mind that their sentences (except for the very shortest ones[2]) are subject to one-third remission for good conduct while in prison. This can be seen by considering the total effective sentences of the sample, i.e. the time (in days) between their first reception into prison under sentence, and their earliest date of release assuming full remission. This information is

---

or can be regarded with it as a single course of conduct: see, e.g. *R.* v. *Torr* [1966] 1 All E.R. 178. In passing it may be noted that these amounts of extra crime are very much greater than among convicted offenders generally. According to the official Criminal Statistics for 1966, there were additional findings of guilt in only 27 per cent of all cases in which men over 21 were convicted of indictable crime in that year; in our sample the proportion is over half.

[1] In a few cases encountered in our concurrent research of fine-defaulters, the difference between first and second sentences was very great indeed: e.g. one man sent to prison for a month for non-payment of a fine for housebreaking was subsequently sentenced to six years for robbery, while another who entered prison for fourteen days in default remained there under a subsequent sentence of four years.

[2] The rule is that remission cannot reduce any prison sentence below 30 days: Prison Rules, 1964 (S.I. No. 388 of 1964), r. 5.

presented in Table III.1; since the mean lengths are somewhat distorted by a small number of very long sentences, the medians are shown as well. It will be seen from this table that the typical 'no option' prisoner in our sample was sentenced, in effect, to spend no more than 133 days in prison; for fine-defaulters the figure is only 30 days.

Table III.1

Effective lengths of sentence, 1966 receptions sample

	*Length of sentence in days**			
	Mean	*S.D.*	*Median*	*N*
Imprisoned without option of a fine for:				
Violence against persons	445·6	322·1	402	18
Robbery	509·4	183·3	460	9
Sexual offences	331·2	206·2	214	11
Breaking offences	339·7	277·2	270	73
Larceny	154·0	140·0	120	77
Fraud, false pretences	276·4	280·2	213	10
Motoring offences	190·5	169·4	121	25
Drunkenness	33·0	4·2	33	2
Other offences	202·1	228·8	127	35
Total, all offences	259·9	247·5	133	260
Imprisoned for non-payment of fines for:				
Violence against persons	90·9	128·2	40	7
Breaking offences	61·2	52·6	40	12
Larceny	43·1	34·9	32	13
Motoring offences	37·6	19·8	32	13
Drunkenness	24·7	6·7	27	53
Other offences	63·5	102·8	30	16
Total, all offences	41·2	55·2	30	114
Total, all men in sample	191·1	160·5	124	374

* From reception under sentence to earliest date of release, assuming full (i.e. one-third) remission.

In addition to information about current offences and sentences, the prison index cards contain some personal and social data. Unfortunately, in collecting information from a variety of sources about our population sample, we found that these data are somewhat inaccurate: in general, they tend to make the prisoners look more respectable, in conventional terms, than they are.[1] This must be

[1] See below, Appendix B, p. 126, n. 1.

borne in mind when comparing receptions with the prison's population in these respects. The mean age of the 'no option' prisoners is just under 30, and the median is 27. The men's latest addresses are mostly in the catchment areas of the courts at which they were convicted: about 40 per cent were living in Birmingham, and an equal number had addresses elsewhere in the West Midlands area. Another 10 per cent were of no fixed abode. About half of the sample were born in Birmingham or the West Midlands; and in terms of nationality, only the Irish are over-represented in the sample in comparison with their numbers in the general population in the West Midlands region. Though adequate comparative data on this point for the general population are not available, the fact that over a quarter of our sample were born outside the West Midlands suggests a fairly high degree of geographical mobility. The men's officially recorded criminal careers support this conclusion: nearly a third of the 'no option' group had been convicted in three or more counties, while one in eight had been convicted in five or more. In terms of place of birth and criminal careers, the men imprisoned for breaking offences and for theft were significantly more mobile geographically than the rest of the sample.[1] Almost half of the sample had never married, and a third of those who had were divorced or legally separated; half of the sample were living in hostels or common lodging-houses. No more than 5 per cent could be placed in the Registrar-General's social classes I or II, on the basis of their occupations according to the prison index.

In demographic terms, the most notable characteristic of the fine-defaulters is the extreme over-representation of men born in Ireland: 43 per cent of the men convicted of drunkenness, and 16·7 per cent of those convicted of other offences came either from Eire or from Northern Ireland. Once this factor is taken into account—the easiest way to do so being to exclude the men convicted of drunkenness from any comparison—the remaining differences between the fine-defaulters and the 'no option' group (in terms of the very crude data available to us) become less marked. Similar proportions were unmarried or separated from their wives; and while the proportion living in lodgings is slightly higher, this is due entirely to the fact that a greater number of the fine-defaulters were convicted in (and

[1] However, even the thieves and housebreakers in our sample have more 'local' criminal careers than the preventive detainees and other persistent offenders studied by Hammond and Chayen: see their book *Persistent Criminals* (1963), pp. 26–28.

living in) the city of Birmingham rather than elsewhere in the West Midlands. Though no less than 73 per cent of the men convicted of drunkenness were described as 'general labourers', the distribution in occupational categories among the remaining fine-defaulters was very close to that of the 'no option' men.

The 'intermediate output' of general local prisons

The composition of the population of the general local prisons differs from that of receptions into prison, since the population is a function not only of the numbers and types of men received, but of the length of time they spend 'inside'. This in turn is determined partly by the sentences imposed by the courts, and partly by the transfer policies which govern the flow of men from general local prisons to institutions of other types—the 'intermediate output' of the general locals.

Of the 374 men in our sample of men received into Winson Green in 1966, about half were transferred to other prisons before being finally discharged; the remainder stayed in Winson Green for the whole of their sentences. However, the probability of being transferred was much greater for some types of inmate than for others. It was significantly higher for 'no option' prisoners than for fine-defaulters, and for those who (*inter alia*) were serving their first or second prison sentences; had fewer than average previous convictions; had not been convicted of drunkenness; were married and not legally separated from their wives; were under 25 on reception into prison; or were recorded as having an occupation other than unskilled manual labour. Of course these factors are not all independent; and some are associated with length of sentence. Moreover, length of sentence itself is positively associated, to a very significant degree, with a high probability of being transferred. Of receptions whose total first sentences were three months or less, just over one-quarter were transferred; at the other extreme, among those serving more than a year the proportion transferred was 85 per cent.[1]

[1] See Table S.4. Of the 167 men in our *population* sample, 67, or 40 per cent, were subsequently transferred to other prisons before being discharged. This figure cannot be directly compared with that of 52 per cent transferred among the receptions, since the population would be expected to contain an over-representation of men destined to spend the whole of their sentences in that institution, and since some of the men in the population had been transferred into Winson Green, having been in other prisons, when we selected them. Making allowance for these factors, however, the experience of our population sample confirms the

Since length of sentence and the probability of being transferred are themselves positively correlated, their effects on the population of the local prisons tend to cancel each other out, to some extent. That they do not do so completely can be illustrated, in a rough and ready way, by comparing the current offences of our sample of receptions into Winson Green prison with the current offences of the population which that prison would be expected to have, if transfer policies had operated in a uniform fashion for all men received; and then comparing this hypothetical population's current offences, in turn, with those of our observed population sample (of 167 men who were actually in the prison on our survey date).[1] The results of this comparison are shown in Table 4. It will be seen that the percentage distribution of current offences among the hypothetical population differs from that among receptions; this difference reflects, roughly, the effect of length of sentence on the composition of the prison population. But the hypothetical population differs in turn from the observed population; and *this* difference mainly reflects the effect of transfer policies. Thus, for example, men under sentence for crimes of violence against the person, who tend to serve fairly long sentences, are over-represented in the hypothetical population relative to receptions. But this over-representation is reduced in our population sample; and this suggests that men sentenced for violence have a greater-than-average probability of being transferred from Winson Green to other prisons. Offenders convicted of drunkenness, motoring and other offences, whose sentences are fairly short, form a smaller fraction of the hypothetical population than of receptions.

---

findings from the receptions sample, especially in respect of the importance of length of sentence: only 15 per cent of those serving a year or less were transferred, against about two-thirds of those serving over a year. The population sample also confirms the tendency of transfer policies to sieve the local prisons' input so far as social class, work habits and work experience are concerned. Of the 24 men in this sample known to have been in non-manual jobs before reception, two-thirds were transferred; of the remainder the proportion transferred was only one-third. Thus of those remaining in Winson Green until discharge, three-fifths were either unemployed or in unskilled manual labouring jobs before reception into prison.

[1] In computing the hypothetical population used in this comparison, I have used the total lengths of sentence (less remission) of the receptions sample; this assumes not only that the probability of transfer is the same for all men received, but also that the time spent in Winson Green before transfer is the same for all who are transferred. In fact, however, there were differences in this respect between those going to open and closed prisons. My calculation also assumes a stationary population (based on a steady flow of receptions at the average level for 1966); thus our population sample, of men actually in the prison on a single day in 1966, may not be truly comparable. See also Appendix C, p. 138 below.

But the first two of these groups form a bigger part of the observed population than of the hypothetical one, since they tend to serve their sentences in the local prison; whereas the opposite appears to be true of those in the miscellaneous category of 'other offences'.

It is important to note, however, that these differences are not simply due to an association between type of current offence and the probability of being transferred. Other factors—in particular length of sentence, and number of previous prison sentences—are more important determinants of transfer policies; and these may lead to differences between the expected and observed populations of the local prison, even in respects which are not themselves

Table III.2

Comparison of percentage distributions of current offences in the Winson Green receptions and population samples, and expected population on assumption of equal transfer rates

Current offence	*Receptions*	*Hypothetical population*	*Observed population*
Violence	6·6	11·1	9·0
Robbery	2·4	5·4	2·4
Heterosexual offences	2·1	3·3	1·8
Homosexual offences	0·8	1·1	1·2
Breaking offences	22·7	32·6	30·5
Larceny	24·2	18·9	28·7
Fraud, false pretences	2·7	3·5	5·4
Motoring offences	10·1	7·9	12·6
Drunkenness	14·7	4·0	6·0
Other offences	13·6	12·2	2·4
Total	100·0	100·0	100·0

The column headed 'Hypothetical population' gives the distribution of current offences which would be expected on the assumptions that:

(a) transfer to other prisons is equally likely for all men received, and
(b) all of those transferred spent the same time in the local prison before being transferred. For the method of calculating this estimated population, see Appendix C, below.

explicitly taken into account in allocation policies or decisions concerning transfers. (These differences will be *consequences* of transfer policies, though not *grounds* of them.)

Similar comparisons illustrating the interaction between length of sentence and transfer policies could be made in respect of other attributes, if more adequate data on receptions were available. In the event, it seems better simply to summarize our data on the population sample, making comparisons with receptions where possible. It should be borne in mind, however, that the composition of the population of a general local prison like Winson Green is in part a function of its output, and not just of the sentences passed by the courts. The consequences of transfer policies for other types of prison will be discussed in the next chapter.

The population of Winson Green prison

In many respects, the population of a general local prison like Winson Green differs from receptions into that prison, in the same ways that those receptions differ from adult offenders convicted by the courts. In terms of current offences, our population's criminality is much more serious than that of the receptions. Violent offences, housebreaking and larceny are more common in the population sample, and drunkenness and other minor offences less common; additional offences and offences taken into consideration are more frequent. Fine-defaulters, who make up a third of Winson Green's input, are much rarer in the prison's population: less than a fifth of the latter group first entered prison for non-payment of fines, and by our survey date half of these men had been produced and given a further sentence without the option of a fine. In all, the proportion produced in this way among the population is nearly three times that among receptions. The average value of property involved was over £100 in more than a third of the current offences of breaking and larceny in the sample.[1]

There is also a marked difference between the reception and population samples in terms of previous recorded crime. This difference is admittedly magnified by the more complete data which we were able to obtain for the population sample. Even allowing for this, however, the population sample's criminal records are very

[1] This may be roughly compared with 6 per cent for all known offences of breaking and larceny known to the police in 1966: see the Criminal Statistics for that year, at p. 7. As would be expected in a group of adults, about half of the property offences of our population sample were committed alone; perhaps surprisingly, there was no significant difference in the value of property involved between crimes committed alone and with others.

much worse than those of men received into Winson Green in 1966 without the option of a fine.[1] While 5 per cent of the population were first offenders, three-quarters of the group had been before the courts on five or more previous occasions (compared with half of the 'no option' receptions); the average number of previous court appearances in the population was nearly ten. In addition to previous occasions convicted, we were able to obtain the number of previous recorded offences—that is, findings of guilt for separate offences, both indictable and non-indictable, plus offences taken into consideration—for the men in the population sample. If we add to this the convictions on the men's current sentences (including additional offences, t.i.c.'s and offences dealt with 'on production' during the current sentence) we arrive at the total number of known crimes for each man in the sample. Since many of these men are dealt with for more than one offence at each court appearance, this figure gives a fairer measure of their criminal behaviour than does the number of occasions on which they have been convicted, though it cannot, of course, reveal how much crime they have committed without being caught. On average, the men in the population sample accounted for nearly 32 known crimes per man.[2] When the sample's time at risk of conviction is taken into account—that is, the time since they attained the minimum age of criminal responsibility, less time spent in institutions—the average 'intensity' of their criminal careers works out at between one and two known crimes for each year at risk. By all of these measures, those under sentence for property offences have much the worst records in the sample. The population sample tended to start their criminal careers slightly earlier than the receptions; still, over a quarter appeared to be 'latecomers' to crime, not convicted before the age of 21.

Table S.2 summarizes the previous penal records of the population sample, and compares with the 'no option' receptions where possible. It will be seen that the proportions having been in young offenders' institutions are similar in the two groups; a higher proportion of the population had previously been on probation, however, nearly a

[1] See Table S.2. The 'no option' men in the receptions sample clearly provide the fairest comparison with the men in the population sample. If the total receptions sample is used, the differences are much greater.

[2] This average is considerably distorted by the small group of men with large numbers of previous offences taken into consideration. However, even if these are excluded, the average is 15·5 known crimes per man; the medians are 13·5 and 14.0, respectively.

third having been dealt with in this way more than once. What really distinguishes the two groups, however, is their previous experience of imprisonment.[1] Over a third of the receptions had apparently not been in prison before; in the population, the corresponding figure is less than a quarter. At the other extreme, only 10 per cent of the men received without the option of a fine had been in prison on five or more previous occasions; among the population the proportion is twice as high.

It is true that, as Glaser has pointed out,[2] nothing whatever can be inferred about the effectiveness of imprisonment from the fact that the majority of men in the prison population have been there before. But the fact that the average population of a prison like Winson Green has such extensive histories of previous imprisonment (in our sample, the median number of previous prison sentences was three) may well give a misleading impression of the criminality of men *received* into prison. My opinion is that in general, the staff of general local prisons have relatively little detailed knowledge of the precise nature of prisoners' criminality; but they do seem to have a general belief (based, perhaps, on the resident population of the institution, with which they have to deal every day) that almost all of the men who enter the prison have been there before (and are, by implication, incorrigible). It would be interesting to know how this belief—which, as we have seen, is incorrect—affects their dealings with the prisoners.[3]

There was little evidence of drug use among our sample: only one man, a registered heroin addict, was serving a sentence for illegal possession of drugs, and only three had previous convictions for this type of offence (all in respect of cannabis). So far as could be

[1] Of the 34 men in this sample classified as 'star' prisoners, three had in fact been in prison before; whereas of the 131 'ordinary' class prisoners, nine had not served a previous prison sentence. Cf. above, p. 18.

[2] See Daniel Glaser, *The Effectiveness of a Prison and Parole System* (Indianapolis: Bobbs-Merrill, 1964), pp. 13–15. We might add that nothing can be inferred about this from the fact that the majority of men *received* into prison have been there before, either.

[3] Two American studies have produced evidence that prison staff members' perceptions of inmates' attitudes tend to impute more anti-social attitudes to the inmates than they in fact possess: see L. E. Hazelrigg, 'An examination of the accuracy and relevance of staff perceptions of the inmate in the correctional institution' (1967), 58 *J. Crim. Law Crim. & P.S.* 204, esp. pp. 209–210; and Stanton Wheeler, 'Role Conflict in Correctional Communities', chap. 6 in D. R. Cressey (ed.), *The Prison* (New York: Holt, Rinehart and Winston, 1961), esp. pp. 237–240. The relations between staff perceptions and institutional populations, regimes or formal goals have not, to my knowledge, been investigated. See further below, pp. 65–69.

ascertained, no more than 8 per cent of the sample had ever used any form of dangerous drugs (including amphetamines).[1]

Alcohol abuse is another matter. No less than 36 per cent of our sample could be described (on the basis of their records, or their own admissions, or both), as heavy drinkers: eight were known to be alcoholics, and a further five had received treatment for alcohol abuse at some time in the past. It could also be established that at least 28 per cent had been drinking heavily, or were actually drunk, at the time of their current offences. While the men's own accounts on this matter could not always be verified by other evidence, they were in general consistent with the facts of the offences themselves. In view of this, it is at first sight surprising that so few of the men had previous convictions for being drunk and disorderly: only 12 per cent, apart from those serving sentences for drunkenness, had apparently ever been in court more than once on this charge. I have already noted that prisoners convicted of drunkenness (usually fine-defaulters) seldom have convictions for anything else; and the converse also appears to be true. In my opinion, selective law enforcement is probably the answer: it is well known that only a small fraction of all public drunkenness leads to a court appearance.

The criminal careers of the men in the population displayed almost exactly the same degree of 'mobility' as those of the receptions: about one-third of those with three or more previous court appearances had been convicted in three or more different counties. However, it must be stressed that this does not mean that these prisoners were 'travelling criminals' who often committed crimes outside the areas in which they lived; indeed, our sample contained only two men whose records (and histories as revealed in our interviews) suggested this. When the numbers of places in which the men had lived for any length of time are taken into account, their careers are seen to be predominantly 'local' in character. Again, the working of the law enforcement process may be partly responsible; 'travelling criminals' are presumably harder to catch. But whatever the cause, the fact

[1] In view of the reported incidence of drug abuse among offenders seen in recent years in borstals and detention centres, however, it is likely that the prison population will change in this respect in the fairly near future. Another factor which may aggravate this problem in English prisons is the recent tendency of some courts to pass long sentences on men convicted of drug 'trafficking': see, e.g. *R.* v. *Blake* [1969] *Crim. L.R.* 609: and on the position in the US Federal prison system, cf. below, p. 72.

remains that nearly half of our sample had never been convicted of a crime outside the 'catchment area' of Winson Green.[1]

The nature of the men's crime is reflected, to a large extent, in their previous prison experience. Of the total number of previous prison sentences served by the population sample (including a few sentences as civil prisoners, and a somewhat larger number as fine-defaulters), nearly three-fifths were served, at least in part, in Winson Green. Even though the men may have been transferred elsewhere for part of their time on these sentences, the familiarity of the majority of our sample with this particular institution is striking. Nearly half of the sample had been in other local prisons during one or more sentences; most of them had done time in at least one other institution. But only 6 per cent of the sample's total previous prison experience (46 out of a total of 777 previous sentences) had included a stay in open prisons, and only 9 per cent had been in closed training or central prisons; less than a quarter of our sample had ever been to either of these types of institution.

Owing to the limitations of our data on receptions into the prison, few direct comparisons can be made between this group and our population sample in respect of social and personal attributes; those which can be made reveal few differences.[2] The age distributions of the two groups are very similar; so are their addresses on reception. In terms of place of birth the two groups are also similar, though the Irish are somewhat less over-represented in the population sample.

[1] About one-quarter of the men in the sample (including over 40 per cent of those who had never married) had lived in seven or more different cities since leaving their parental homes. It is important to note, however, that this geographically mobile group were not necessarily vagrants: only three of the sample, so far as we could determine, were actually 'sleeping rough' prior to reception, and only five of those whom we interviewed would admit that they had ever done so. Again, length of sentence appears to be the answer: the 'stage army' of tramps, alcoholics, etc. are seldom in prison for more than a month or so, and thus make up only a small part of the prison's resident population. This is not to minimize the wider problem of homelessness and social isolation which confronts prison welfare officers. Over a quarter of those for whom we could obtain information said they had no place to go on discharge from prison; the true number is likely to have been higher. Cf. the National Assistance Board report on Homeless Single Persons (London: HMSO, 1966), esp. pp. 58, 94, 125, 159, on the prison experience of men in common lodging-houses, hostels and reception centres, and men 'sleeping rough'.

[2] In many respects in which they can be compared, our population sample is reasonably similar to the Pentonville population surveyed by Morris and Morris in 1959. Such differences as appear can for the most part be plausibly explained by regional differences (London versus the West Midlands), transfer policies and the fact that almost all of the input to Pentonville in 1959 consisted of recidivist prisoners. See T. and P. Morris, *Pentonville* (1963), chap. 3.

A higher proportion of the population (just under half) were married, though the proportions divorced or legally separated are about the same in the two groups. However, about a third of the married men, though not legally separated, were living apart from their wives. As might be expected, there were significant differences in marital status and stability between the star and ordinary prisoners; the former were less likely to be separated or divorced or living apart, had been married longer on average, and so on.[1] But there were no significant differences in the *criminal* records of the married, separated or divorced and unmarried men, either in terms of previous court appearances, or previous convictions per year at risk.

Among those in our sample who were married and living with their wives, contacts with the families through letters and visits were generally well maintained during their sentences; most had sent and received the maximum permitted letters and visiting orders, and had received visits on every occasion in which an order was sent. Nor was there any evidence of changes in these men's marital situations as a result of their time in prison up to our survey data; in the few cases in which legal separation or divorce took place in that period, the prisoner had not been living with his wife before he entered prison.[2]

A certain amount of information about early life could be obtained for 147 of the 167 men in the sample. Of this group, 88 men (60 per cent) came from homes which were structurally intact (both natural parents, living together) until the prisoners had reached at least the age of 14. A further 9 per cent had been raised by one natural parent and a step-parent; a similar proportion had been brought up by other relatives owing to the absence of one or more natural parents. A fifth of the sample had been brought up by one natural parent alone, or had been in institutions, fostered, or adopted; and in the

[1] Making allowance for the difference in composition of samples, our data agree closely with those of P. Morris, *Prisoners and their Families* (London: Allen and Unwin, 1965), p. 31.

[2] It must be remembered, however, that in most cases this time was very short. Moreover, almost all of the married men in our sample were living either in the city of Birmingham itself, or elsewhere in the West Midlands; it was thus comparatively simple for their families to visit them. But (chiefly because they had less previous prison experience) the married men who were transferred were slightly more likely than single men to be sent to open prisons located some distance from their homes; for some of these men, visits may well have been less frequent during the later months of their sentence. Even in the long term, however, there is evidence that the effect of imprisonment on the prisoner's marriage is not necessarily adverse, and may be just the opposite: See P. Morris, *op. cit.*, pp. 280–289.

overwhelming majority of these cases, the home had been broken by divorce or separation. This proportion of men from 'broken' homes (especially those caused by divorce or separation) is undoubtedly higher than in the general population;[1] but in this respect —as in most others—the Winson Green population is a good deal less abnormal than the preventive detainees and other English persistent adult offenders studied by West,[2] Hammond[3] and Taylor.[4]

Two further things distinguish the backgrounds of Winson Green's population from these 'habitual prisoners'. First, no more than a fifth of our sample had a known history of mental treatment of any kind, at any time in their lives. Among those in our sample who had undergone such treatment, the commonest reason was alcoholism; the next most frequent diagnostic label, mentioned in the records of six men, was 'depression', usually in connection with a suicide attempt. The men's present mental states (at the time of our survey) revealed an even lower prevalence of known abnormality: only 10 per cent had been clinically described, either in court reports or by prison doctors after reception, as being abnormal in any way (and half of these had received nothing more than the label 'psychopath'). These figures must obviously be taken as absolute minimum estimates of psychiatric abnormality in our sample; still, it appears from the available evidence that the prevalence of mental illness in the local prisons' population is less than that found by West.[5]

The 'black sheep' phenomenon was also less common in our sample. West, in considering the family backgrounds of persistent offenders, found that about one-sixth came from families in which some other member had apparently been in trouble with the law.[6] But over one-third of our sample had parents or siblings (or, in a few cases, both) who had also been convicted on one or more occasions; there was, not surprisingly, a strong association between this

[1] For a recent review of English research on this subject, see C. Banks, 'Boys in Detention Centres', in C. Banks and P. L. Broadhurst, *Stephanos: Studies in Psychology presented to Cyril Burt* (London: University of London Press, 1965), pp. 173–205, at pp. 183–190.

[2] D. J. West, *The Habitual Prisoner* (London: Macmillan, 1963), pp. 12–19.

[3] W. H. Hammond and E. Chayen, *Persistent Criminals* (London: HMSO, 1963), pp. 150–151.

[4] R. S. Taylor, 'The Habitual Criminal: Observations on some of the Characteristics of Men Sentenced to Preventive Detention', (1960) 1 *Brit. J. Criminol.* 21.

[5] D. J. West, *op. cit.*, Chap. VI; but cf. Appendix D, p. 141, for a counter-example.

[6] West, *op. cit.*, p. 16.

attribute and a record of juvenile delinquency, and convictions per year at risk.

Nearly 40 per cent of our sample were unemployed immediately prior to reception into the prison. Of the remainder, almost one-third were in unskilled manual work, and half were in either skilled or semi-skilled manual work; almost all of the rest were either employed in minor clerical, supervisory or sales jobs, or else were self-employed (as car salesmen, general dealers, etc.). Only one man (predictably, an embezzler) had held a managerial job. The men's work statuses immediately before reception, or at the time of their crimes, may admittedly be misleading as to their usual work, since some of the sample had lost or quit their jobs (for one reason or another) just before committing the offences which led them to prison.[1]

Moreover, many of the men had had only short periods at liberty since their last discharge from prison—the median time was seven months—and, like most recidivist prisoners, their work histories were very uneven, so there was very little point in asking what kind of work they *usually* did. Instead, we sought to discover the *highest* class of legitimate work which they had ever done. Just over half of the men for whom this information could be obtained had held a skilled or semi-skilled job at *some* time in their lives; but about 30 per cent had never done anything other than unskilled manual work.

Half of the men whom we interviewed claimed to have held a job for two years or longer at some time in their working lives. Usually, however, this job (when it could be verified) turned out to have been several years previously, and was seldom the highest class of job the prisoner had ever held; not infrequently it was a period of apprenticeship or similar work not long after leaving school. Only a quarter of the sample had been in their last job a year or longer, and one in six had been unemployed continuously since their last discharge from prison (including ten men who had been unemployed for six months or more). At the other extreme, in the same period of time, a similar proportion had had three or more jobs.

Data on the occupations of the men's fathers (or, in a few cases,

[1] Of those who were employed just before conviction, over 80 per cent knew or believed that they had lost their jobs, usually (but not necessarily) as a result of their crime or sentence. By their own accounts, those men who were working prior to reception into prison were making fairly good money; the median net income from all sources was £24. But the reliability of these figures is suspect; and an unknown fraction of this income was the proceeds of crime.

stepfathers) could be obtained for 124 cases. While—owing to missing data—direct comparison of father's occupation and son's highest occupation was possible in only 77 of these cases, there was nonetheless clear evidence of downward mobility: almost half of the prisoners had never held jobs at the same level of skill as their fathers. Our data show, as might be expected, an association between downward mobility and previous criminality and prison experience. In addition, though the numbers are small, there is a difference in intergenerational mobility between those who had criminal parents or siblings, and those who did not: the first group are much more likely to have moved either upward or downward, than the second.

Length of residence in Winson Green

We have seen that two factors—length of sentence, and transfer policies—affect the composition of the local prison population. Broadly speaking, the younger prisoners convicted of more serious offences, serving longer sentences and without the option of a fine, but with fewer previous convictions (especially for indictable crimes) and relatively little previous prison experience, were more likely to be sent to other prisons. Those retained at Winson Green consequently contained a majority of the fine-defaulters, almost all the men convicted of drunkenness, and relatively high proportions of unmarried, unsettled men, with many previous convictions and lengthy records of previous imprisonment, who were unemployed or in unskilled labouring jobs on reception into the prison. A final factor to be taken into account is the length of time which the men who were transferred spent in Winson Green before going to another type of prison; and, related to this, the proportions of their total effective sentences which these men spent in the local prison.

The data concerning our sample of receptions show that in most cases, transfers came fairly soon after first reception into the prison, for those who left Winson Green at all; three-quarters of all those transferred had left within a month. But it was noticeable that those transferred to closed prisons stayed longer in the local prison than those who went to open prisons. Only a third of them had left within a month, and a few were there for over six months; one man did not leave for over a year. When these figures are related to the length of time the men had left to serve, however, the picture looks a bit more favourable even for those sent to closed institutions;

only 15 per cent of these men spent more than a fifth of their sentences in Winson Green. The net result is that the distribution of the proportions of total effective sentence spent in Winson Green is roughly U-shaped. For all categories of current offence (except drunkenness, for which there were very few transfers), about as many men in each category were transferred out after spending 20 per cent of their sentences or less, as remained in Winson Green for the whole of their sentences. This—plus the short sentences received by the majority of the men in our receptions sample—helps to explain the fact that 55 per cent of the sample were in Winson Green for less than one month, and another 20 per cent had left by the end of two months. The mean length of residence for the whole group was 30 days, and only 7 per cent of the group remained in the prison for over six months.

In the population sample, those men who were transferred spent almost as long in Winson Green as the men who remained there until discharge: the median lengths of time were 113 and 121 days, respectively. As with the receptions sample, however, a more favourable picture emerges when the total length of time these men had to serve on their current sentences is taken into account. On average, the effective sentences of the men transferred were much longer than those of the group discharged. Consequently, on average they only spent about one-quarter of their total sentences in Winson Green, whereas the group discharged from that prison (apart from the few who had been transferred in) naturally spent the whole of their sentences there. Predictably, the star prisoners spent the least time in the prison: the median time was 49 days, against 128 for the ordinaries. For the whole of the population sample, the average time spent in Winson Green was just over five months.

This average conceals some wide variations, however; and it must not be forgotten that a small proportion of all men who enter local prisons remain there for what are, relatively speaking, very long periods of time. Data concerning our receptions sample suggest that about 10 per cent of all men received under sentence without the option of a fine will remain in the local prison for over six months, and that about 1 per cent of all receptions will be there for over a year. In terms of the actual numbers received into Winson Green in 1966, these percentages refer to about 260 and 26 men, respectively: and it can be estimated that these men would account for about 30 per cent and 7 per cent, respectively, of the population under sentence at any time. These estimates are supported by the fact that in our population sample there were 36 men, or over a fifth of the sample, who on their current sentences spent between six and nine months in Winson Green; and a further 15 men who were there for a year or more.

Our sample of the prison's population can in fact be stratified into three groups of roughly equal size, according to the lengths of time they spent in that prison. The first of these groups—short-term residents, as they may be called—spent less than two months in Winson Green. The second—the medium-term residents—stayed more than two months, but less than six months; the third group, the long-term residents, remained longer than six months. (These three groups of inmates are compared in Table S.3.) The short-term group contains about the expected proportions of violent and sexual offenders; but while some of these men have committed quite serious offences, and are serving long sentences, they are fairly quickly transferred to other institutions. Housebreakers are slightly under-represented in this group; men convicted of drunkenness, motoring and other (usually rather minor) offences, who tend to serve short terms and who are less often transferred, are over-represented. Among the long-term residents, by contrast, violent offenders are very much over-represented, as are housebreakers; thieves are under-represented. In terms of prisoner types the effect of this stratification is even more striking: whereas nearly half of the short-term residents are star prisoners, such men make up only about 6 per cent of those remaining in the prison for more than six months.

These differences may well be important in relation to the social organization of the institution, and relations between inmates and staff. I have already suggested that the composition of the average population of a prison like Winson Green may affect the staff's perceptions of the characteristics of receptions into prison; clearly, stereotypes formed in this way may be especially biassed if they are based on the long-term residents of the institution, with whom the staff have the longest continuous contact. Where relations among inmates are concerned, the position is less clear. Given the extreme physical constraints on association between inmates in overcrowded general local prisons at the present time, and the short sentences of the majority of prisoners, the opportunities for the development of an inmate social system, stable social roles, etc., is probably fairly limited. In any case, there is some reason to think that the oppositional inmate culture described by Gresham Sykes and other American writers[1] is less marked in penal institutions outside the United States.[2] Moreover, as the illustrative cases described in Appendix D[3] suggest, the majority of the long-term residents of Winson Green do not appear to fulfil the traditional criteria of leadership among prison inmates.[4] Against this, we have seen that the majority of the men in general local prisons have been in prison before, and that many have been in the same prison on several previous occasions; undoubtedly, many of them were well acquainted before beginning their sentences, as well as sharing the values of a criminal subculture outside the prison. In this situation, the influence of the longer-term residents of the prison on the informal social system of the general local prison may be substantial. Further research on this point is clearly needed.

[1] G. Sykes, *The Society of Captives* (Princeton, N.J.: Princeton University Press, 1958), esp. chap. 5; G. Sykes and S. L. Messinger, 'The Inmate Social System', in G. Grosser (ed.), *Theoretical Studies in the Social Organization of the Prison* (New York: Social Science Research Council, 1960), chap. 1.

[2] Cf. T. and P. Morris, *Pentonville*, *op. cit.*, chap. XI; T. Mathiesen, *The Defences of the Weak* (London: Tavistock, 1965), esp. pp. 137–140.

[3] See below, pp. 138–144.

[4] See, e.g., C. Schrag, 'Leadership Among Prison Inmates', (1954) 19 *Am. Social Rev.*, 37; G. Sykes, *op. cit.*, pp. 99–104; P. G. Garabedian, 'Social Roles in a Correctional Community', (1964) 55 *J. Crim. Law., Crim. & Pol. Sci.*, 338; Morris and Morris, *op. cit.*, pp. 241–53; D. Clemmer, *The Prison Community*, chap. 6.

IV

Estimates Concerning the Rest of the System

It must be emphasized again that the preceding chapter described the input, population and output of *one* type of English prison only. While large general local prisons like Winson Green are, in quantitative terms alone, an important part of the English prison system, they are by no means the whole of that system. In this chapter we shall consider further how the general local prisons fit into the rest of the system, and try to get some idea of the composition of the populations of other types of prison and of the system as a whole. Ideally, for this purpose similar surveys should be carried out at special local, training and central prisons; perhaps, as the system develops in future years, it will be desirable for some purposes to sub-divide the system still further, and consider separately each prison within these categories providing a different regime and dealing with a different type of offender. The prison index now being developed by the Home Office should make it possible to obtain some information of this kind.[1] Meanwhile, some estimates can be made, using the official statistics of receptions into prison (published annually by the Home Office), together with the data from the Winson Green survey and other sources.

Empirical evidence on transfer policies

As we have seen, about half of the 374 men in our sample of receptions into Winson Green in 1966 were transferred to other prisons before being discharged on completion of their sentences. Our data concerning these transfers must be interpreted in the light of the number of institutions available, and the extent of overcrowding, in the West

[1] See RPD (1968), p. 2; for a study illustrating the inter-institutional differences which may exist in a similar system see R. Cockett, 'Borstal Training: A Follow-up Study', (1967) 7 *Brit. J. Criminol.*, 150.

Midlands at the time of our research. When this is done, the data tend broadly to confirm the transfer policies described in Chapter II.

Since 1967, when the administration of the English prison system was put on a regional basis, it has been the intention that prisoners should in general serve their sentences within the region in which they entered the system, rather than being transferred to another part of the country. But this policy had not been implemented at the time of our research[1] and most of the men in our sample of receptions who were under long sentences had to be sent to closed central prisons—Dartmoor, Parkhurst, or Wakefield—a considerable distance from their homes. There was no closed training prison in the Midland area until July 1966, when Gartree prison, near Market Harborough in Leicestershire, was opened. There was a closed special local prison at Stafford; and three open prisons, Drake Hall (a special local), Ashwell and Sudbury (training prisons).

Data concerning our sample of receptions are summarized in Table S.4. It will be seen that just over half of those transferred, in this sample, went to open prisons. The majority of these men, however, were short-term star prisoners sent to Drake Hall: this special local 'satellite' of Winson Green thus took about 40 per cent of all receptions who were transferred. The next largest group—about a quarter of all those transferred—went to the closed special local prison at Stafford: most of these men were also short-term stars. The remainder of those transferred went to other closed prisons: their numbers were about evenly divided between those going to other general local prisons (some as far afield as Exeter), and those going to closed training or central prisons. As would be expected, men convicted of sexual or violent offences, and those serving longer sentences for property crimes, were much less likely to be sent to open institutions: in our sample, the probability of reaching an open prison during a sentence for such a crime was about one in sixteen.[2] Owing to the limitations of our data, and the smallness of the sample, very little can be said about the men transferred to closed prisons, except that as a group they were much less likely to be serving their

[1] It is not likely to be fully implemented, in fact, for some time: see Cmnd. 4214, pp. 67–75. A new closed prison for 500 men is to be opened at Long Lartin in Worcestershire in 1971; in addition, one section of a new prison in Oxfordshire is to be a training prison for 300 men. Long-sentence prisoners in the region will then presumably be sent to Gartree, which is to become a Category A (maximum-security) prison.

[2] A previous record of this type of crime did not, in our sample, absolutely disqualify men for allocation to open conditions.

first prison sentences than men transferred to open institutions. The experience of our sample on this point is consistent with earlier evidence on the use of open prisons: for star prisoners the chance of going to an open institution was just less than one half, and for ordinaries it was about one in seven.[1] It is also of interest to note that three-fifths of those in our sample who were transferred to closed central prisons were known to have previous convictions for violent or sexual crime.

The more detailed data relating to our population sample confirm the findings from the receptions sample, in relation to the types of offenders sent to other prisons of different kinds. Thus, of the 67 men in this sample who were transferred, nine—all of them classified as star prisoners—went to Drake Hall open prison. One of these men had been convicted of assault on a police officer, and was transferred back to Winson Green; the remainder had committed property or motoring offences, and were serving sentences of six months or less. Five men—three of them stars, with records of sexual or violent offences in the past—went to Stafford. The biggest group—23 men, or just over a third of those transferred—went to the closed training prison at Gartree: none of these men was a star. Ashwell open prison took ten of the men transferred, of whom seven were ordinaries; this is consistent with the policy noted earlier, of mixing star and recidivist property offenders in this prison. Four men, all of them stars convicted of property offences, went to Sudbury open prison; three men (one of them a star, subsequently sent to an open prison in the North of England) were transferred to other closed local prisons. Finally, thirteen of the sample transferred went to central prisons. This group included two men convicted of wounding, one convicted of incest, and four convicted of robbery. The data also confirm the over-riding importance of a current offence or previous record of sexual or violent crime, in tending to disqualify men for allocation to open conditions; in fact, no man in our population

[1] According to Home Office evidence to the Royal Commission on the Penal System, of the men seen at general local prisons in 1964, 60 per cent of the stars and 17·5 per cent of the ordinaries were considered to be 'suitable' for open conditions. However, only 45·7 per cent of the stars and 13·5 per cent of the ordinaries were actually sent to open prisons, owing 'less to lack of vacancies than to other factors . . . such as medical reasons, the domestic circumstances of the prisoner . . . and the shortness of the sentence.' Royal Commission on the Penal System in England and Wales: Written Evidence from Government Departments, Miscellaneous Bodies and Individual Witnesses. Volume I: Government Departments. (London: HMSO, 1967), pp. 88–90 ('Supplementary Note by the Home Office on the use of open prisons.')

sample who was sent to an open prison was known ever to have committed such a crime.

What we could *not* establish, from our data, was any clear distinction in respect of work habits and experience, marital situation or any other personal or social factor, between the men sent to the closed training prison (Gartree) and men serving similar sentences who were retained in Winson Green. Those transferred to the training prison had fewer previous convictions and less previous prison experience; but no other evidence of 'trainability' emerged from a comparison of the two groups. I would stress that this does not necessarily mean that there were in fact no differences between these groups, which would have justified transferring the one and retaining the other; merely that we could not discover any such differences from our data, apart from generally shorter criminal and prison records. However, there are two possible reasons for this, apart from the smallness of our sample. First, Gartree prison was only opened in July 1966, and was filled in the first instance by a bulk transfer of men from Winson Green who were certainly not selected for their 'trainability'; it may well be that more discriminating allocation policies were introduced after the men in our samples were transferred. Secondly, it is possible that of all those men who—in view of their criminality, work habits, etc.—might reasonably be classified as 'trainable' and sent to prisons such as Gartree, only a fraction can now be accommodated in prisons such as Gartree. This would have the result that the men remaining in general local prisons for the whole of their sentences, though generally less 'trainable', nonetheless contained a fairly large group of prisoners who could be sent to training prisons if sufficient space existed in them. In my opinion, it is likely that this is true. If so, however, it casts considerable doubt on the official claim that 'all suitable prisoners now receive training', which was one ground for abolishing the special sentence of corrective training.[1] One justification for this sentence was precisely that men given it were much more likely to serve their time in training prisons than similar men sentenced to ordinary imprisonment for the same length of time.[2]

A final question remaining to be answered concerning transfer policies concerns the number of prisoners transferred more than once

[1] See the White Paper *The Adult Offender* (Cmnd. 2852 of 1965), para 10.
[2] For a discussion of this point see A. E. Bottoms, 'Toward a Custodial Training Sentence for Adults' [1965] *Crim. L. R.* 582, at pp. 585–586.

during their sentences. In an effort to answer this question, we selected a 10 per cent sample of men received into Winson Green in 1963, and obtained information about them from their prison records. Unfortunately, the value of these data is limited by the large proportion of men (almost 15 per cent of those received under sentence) whose records could not be obtained, since the very fact that the records were untraceable suggests that these prisoners may have moved around more than those for whom information was available. Moreover, the prison system was somewhat different in the earlier period: while there was slightly less overcrowding, there was no closed training prison in the Midland region in 1963, so that prisoners were likely to have to be transferred further afield if they were transferred at all, and a much higher proportion went to other local prisons than in 1966.

Our data show, however, that an overwhelming majority of the men transferred in this sample, both to open and to closed prisons, went to one institution only. As in 1966, the largest share of men transferred from Winson Green went to Drake Hall open prison; most of these were short-term star prisoners. It appears that about 5 per cent of those sent to open prisons were found to be unsuitable for this type of institution and returned to Winson Green, or sent to another closed prison. This suggests that the effective transfer rate to these prisons (as revealed by our 1966 receptions sample) should probably be reduced somewhat.[1] Against this, however, the table shows that a minority of the men moved from Winson Green to other closed prisons were subsequently transferred to open prisons before being finally discharged. A small group of men, all sent to closed training or central prisons, were transferred to two or more other prisons first, for short periods of time; but on the available evidence there is no reason to believe that the number of prisoners moved more than twice during their sentences is large.

Estimates of the total prison population

Let us now see what estimates can be made concerning the total population of men under sentence for criminal offences in the

[1] Cf. the evidence referred to in n. 1, p. 51: of prisoners received at open prisons in 1964, 10·5 per cent of the stars and 16·5 per cent of the ordinaries were subsequently found to be unsuitable for open conditions—'in most cases because they absconded or otherwise offended against discipline'—and were returned to closed prisons.

English prison system as a whole. A reasonable first step in this process is to estimate the numbers in the total prison population who are serving sentences of different lengths. Until 1 April 1968—when parole was introduced by the Criminal Justice Act 1967—prison sentences in England were almost all 'determinate' or 'definite' in length. That is, the maximum time that the prisoner could be confined was fixed in advance, by the sentencing court; and the minimum time he would serve was fixed, by law, at a definite fraction of that maximum. Prisoners were entitled to remission of one-third of their sentences unless they misbehaved while in captivity, subject to the rule that remission could not reduce any sentence to less than one month. This is still the rule for the majority of men received into English prisons, since prisoners do not become eligible for parole until they have served one-third of their sentence or at least one year.[1] Thus men sentenced to eighteen months or less—who constitute about 90 per cent of receptions under sentence in any year—are not eligible for parole at all; and in practice, at least up to now, only a minority of those serving longer sentences have actually been released on parole even though they have been technically eligible for it.[2] Thus for the majority of prisoners the effective length of sentence is about two-thirds of the length fixed by the courts.

Of course, some men do lose part of their remission, and therefore serve more than two-thirds of their sentences; indeed, one man in Winson Green in 1966 had managed to lose all of his remission, though such cases are exceptional. Furthermore, as was noted in Chapter III, a small proportion—of the order of 5–6 per cent—of men received under sentence are produced in court again and given a further sentence;[3] these sentences on production are not shown in the Prison Department's annual statistics, which accordingly underestimate slightly the effective lengths of sentences actually served. Against this, about 20–25 per cent of the fine-defaulters (and civil prisoners) in our 1966 sample of receptions into Winson Green paid the amounts they owed, and were accordingly discharged from prison, often after serving only a few days; a smaller proportion paid

[1] Criminal Justice Act 1967, s. 60 (1). Thus, for example, a man sentenced to three years may be released on parole after one year, but in any case will normally be released after two.

[2] See below, pp. 75–76.

[3] See above, p. 31; the proportion produced among fine-defaulters was about one in nine.

a part of what they owed, thus reducing their sentences, before being discharged. On balance, then, as a very rough estimate of the overall effective length of prison sentences, we may take about 70 per cent of the length of sentences imposed by the courts and shown in the Prison Department's statistics—bearing in mind that this average probably conceals some fairly wide variations among different groups of prisoners.

A group for which the effective length of sentence probably varies considerably, and for which it cannot be so easily reckoned, consists of men under sentence of 'life' imprisonment, or detained 'during Her Majesty's Pleasure'. According to the White Paper *People in Prison*, 'the term of imprisonment actually served by prisoners sentenced for life is determined according to the circumstances of every particular case—and every case is different'.[1] In practice, in the immediate post-war years, the majority of reprieved murderers (automatically sentenced to life imprisonment) served seven or eight years;[2] but during the past two decades the average period has apparently lengthened slightly. Of 180 life sentence prisoners released in the ten years 1959–69, all but 19 had served for periods equivalent to a fixed sentence of 10½ years or longer, on which the normal one-third remission had been granted: on average that is rather more than nine years.[3] However, a few individuals have remained in prison for very much longer periods; and there have been several official statements in recent years to the effect that the actual length of a life sentence for murder may increase still further in future.[4] In practice, for the period 1950–68, an average effective length of ten years for all males imprisoned for life seems to give a reasonably good estimate of their numbers in the prison population. But it must be borne in mind that this average figure may well be too low, in future years.

Given the average effective lengths of sentences, the composition of the prison population by length of sentence can be estimated from official statistics of receptions, by a simple formula.[5] I have made

[1] Cmnd. 4214, p. 19.

[2] See the Report of the Royal Commission on Capital Punishment (Cmnd. 8932 of 1953), paras 644–646, and Table 12, Appendix 3; see also the Home Office evidence to the Commission, esp. paras 35–48.

[3] Cmnd. 4214, *loc. cit.*; detailed figures are published in a Written Answer by the Home Secretary, on 22 April 1970, in H.C. Deb., vol. 800, No. 101, at p. 115.

[4] See, for example, the report of the Home Office Advisory Council on the Penal System, *The Regime for Long-Term Prisoners in Conditions of Maximum Security* (London: HMSO, 1968), paras 16, 17.

[5] The method is described in Appendix C, pp. 133–136. Similar work on this

estimates, using this method, of the year-end populations of men serving sentences of ordinary imprisonment, for the years 1950–67; the results, for the beginning and end of this period, are shown in Figure 1. These estimates include fine-defaulters, but exclude men serving sentences of corrective training and preventive detention;

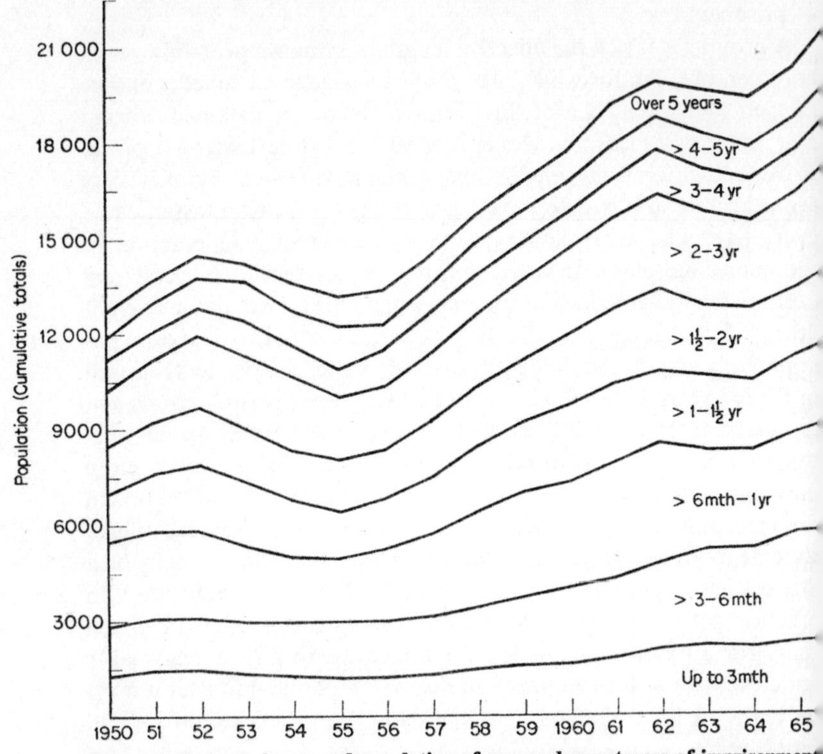

Figure 1. Estimated year end population of men under sentences of imprisonmen 1950–1967 (cumulative totals).

the effects of these measures, which have now been abolished, wi be discussed in the next chapter. It will be seen that, in terms o lengths of sentence, the composition of the male population unde sentences of ordinary imprisonment has remained fairly stable ove

problem has been done independently by Dr Charlotte Banks. See her pape 'Prison Receptions and Population', presented at the Third National Conferenc on Research and Teaching in Criminology, Cambridge Institute of Criminolog July 1968 (mimeo). For an earlier use of the same method see my article, 'Custodi Training Sentences: Another View' (1966), *Crim. L.R.* 84, at n. 94.

this period. Between 20 and 25 per cent of the population is serving sentences of six months or less; about half is under sentence of 18 months or less; another quarter is serving sentences of over 18 months up to three years. But Figure 1 reveals clearly the impact of length of sentence on the population of the prison system: men serving sentences of over three years, though they constitute only 2–3 per cent of annual *receptions* under sentence, made up no less than a fifth of the population of males under sentence at the end of 1967.

Moreover, this analysis reveals that there was a substantial increase throughout the 1960's of the proportion of men in the prison population who were serving sentences of over five years. Figure 2 shows three-year moving averages of receptions under sentence of five years or more, in 1950–66, and the estimated year-end populations of these long-sentence men in the same years. In each case, the overall trends are fairly steadily upward throughout the period, with especially sharp upturns in the last three or four years: the population of long-sentence men (over five years) went up by about one and a half times during a time when the total male prison population increased by less than 60 per cent. By the end of 1967, there must have been nearly 2,000 men in prison in England and Wales who were serving sentences of ordinary imprisonment of over five years. Of this number, about 30 per cent were serving 'life' sentences.[1]

The causes of this increase in the long-sentence population are not difficult to identify. First, there has been a definite tendency for the courts to impose much longer fixed-term sentences for a few types of serious crime—in particular, for 'professional' armed robbery of large sums of money. Crimes of this kind were increasing, even before the so-called Great Train Robbery in 1963;[2] and while many of those

[1] The discussion of this problem in the White Paper *People in Prison* (*op. cit.*, pp. 18–19) seems somewhat misleading. It is stated that 'the number of *fixed* entences of ten years and over has not changed greatly during the decade', hough it is conceded that 'there has been a change in the number of offenders vith fixed sentences of 14 years and over.' In fact, though the absolute numbers of eceptions of *over* ten years are too small to permit any analysis of trends, there as certainly been an increase in this group since 1960, particularly in the years 963–1967; the average in that five-year period was 20·8 per year, against 10·2 n the preceding five years. Moreover, as Figure 2 shows, receptions under entence of over seven years up to (and *including*) ten years have risen almost as teeply in the same period, from an annual average of 39 in 1958–62, to 63·2 in 963–67. Since 1960 the year-end populations in these three groups taken ogether have roughly doubled, and in the case of fixed-term sentences of over en years must have tripled.

[2] *R.* v. *Wilson and others* [1965] 1 Q.B. 402 (sentences of up to 30 years upheld on ppeal). For a discussion of trends in robbery in the years to 1960 see F. H. IcClintock and E. Gibson, *Robbery in London* (London: Macmillan, 1961), sp. pp. 73–85, 96–120.

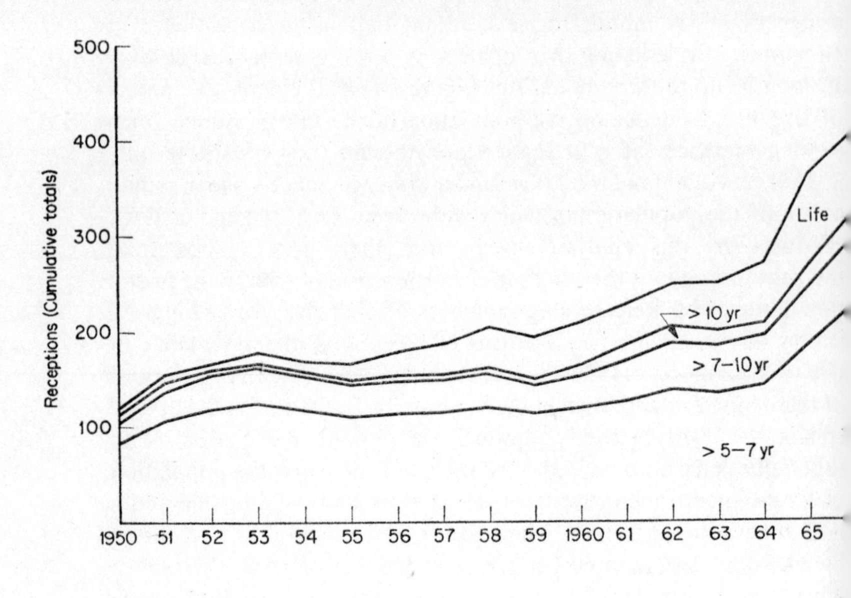

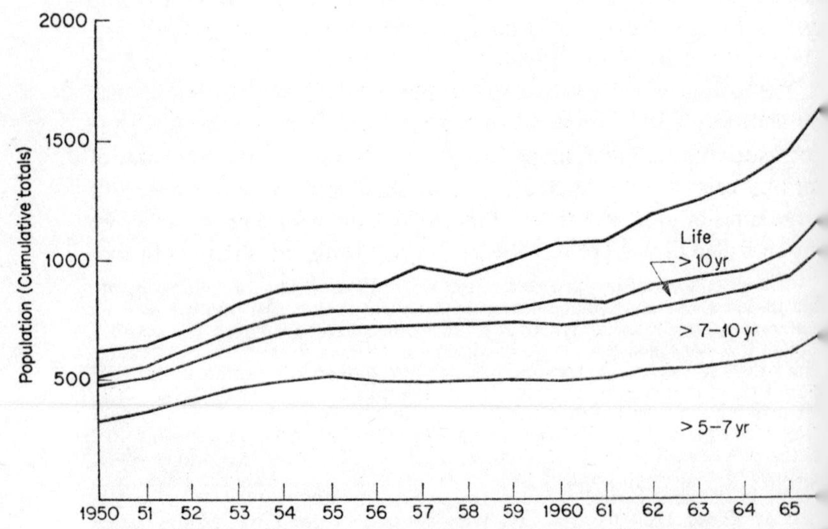

Figure 2. Receptions under sentence (top) and estimated year end population (bottom), adult male prisoners (cumulative totals).

responsible for these crimes are not caught or convicted, the sentences normally passed on those who are convicted have increased substantially.[1] Secondly, since 1957 the courts have used life imprisonment (and in a few instances long fixed-term sentences) in cases of manslaughter on the ground of 'diminished responsibility'—cases some of which, in earlier years, would probably have resulted in verdicts of insanity and detention in hospital rather than in prison.[2] Thirdly, in this period there has been a slight, though increasing, tendency for the courts to use life imprisonment for persons convicted of very serious violent or sexual offences, who appear to be mentally unstable though unsuitable for psychiatric treatment, and potentially dangerous.[3] Another important factor contributing to the growth of the long-sentence prison population in the past decade was the *de facto* abolition of capital punishment during that period. As a result of this, the number of receptions under sentence of life imprisonment (including commuted death sentences) has risen steadily; by the end of 1968 there were nearly 600 men in prison serving 'life' sentences, a number of whom would, in earlier years, have been hanged.

The composition of the population by current offence

Let us now attempt to estimate, in the same way, the composition of the prison population in terms of the current offences for which that population is imprisoned. This can be done reasonably accurately, since statistics of receptions into prison, by current offence and length of sentence, are now published in the Prison Department's annual reports. These statistics group receptions, for each category of current offence, into eleven groups by length of sentence. Using these data, separate estimates have been made for twelve categories of current offence, as follows: murder; other offences of violence

[1] Compare, e.g., *R.* v. *Butt* (1957) 41 *Cr. App. R.* 82 (four years), with *R.* v *Curbishley* [1964] *Crim. L.R.* 555 (fifteen years). For a full discussion of judicial sentencing policy in these cases see D. A. Thomas, *Principles of Sentencing* (London: Heinemann, 1970), pp. 54 and 44. Unfortunately, neither the official Criminal Statistics nor the Prison Department's statistics fully reveal the extent of this change in policy, first because all sentences of over ten years are lumped together in each series, and secondly because in the Prison Department's figures before 1968 robbery is included in a miscellaneous category of 'other' indictable offences.

[2] On this point see E. Gibson and S. Klein, *Murder, 1957 to 1968* (London: HMSO, 1969), Chap. 3; and for a discussion of cases up to 1964 see (1964) 27 M.L.R. 9, at pp. 24–33.

[3] See D. A. Thomas, *op. cit.*, pp. 272–279, for some examples.

against the person; buggery and other indictable homosexual offences; rape and other indictable heterosexual offences; house-breaking; aggravated larceny; simple larceny; receiving; frauds and false pretences; other indictable offences (including robbery); all offences akin to indictable offences; and all non-indictable offences. Unfortunately, this series of statistics only extends back to 1960; and figures of receptions for at least twelve years would be necessary to make complete estimates of the population (including the important group of long-sentence prisoners). Unpublished figures for 1959 were provided by the Home Office;[1] even so, in a few cases some guesses had to be made about the numbers in some of the longest sentence groups. The estimates for the end of 1967 are shown in Table S.6, which shows the composition of the male prison population by length of sentence and current offence.

The most striking thing to emerge from these estimates is the impact of the association between current offences of violence, and long sentences. Of the 2,000 or so men in prison at the end of 1967 who were serving sentences of over five years, nearly 75 per cent had been imprisoned for an offence of violence against the person (including murder) or a serious sexual offence; even if murderers are excluded, violent crime accounts for over half the men in this long-sentence group. The concentration of violence and serious sexual crime appears to be even greater among the group serving sentences of over seven years, virtually all of whom are 'inside' for a current offence of one of these types. In contrast, among men serving sentences of less than three years, offenders against property predominate: violent and sexual offenders constitute only about 15 per cent of this group.

The most important factor affecting the prison population during the years 1960–67, of course, was the increase in the total number of receptions under sentence. But it is important to note that the increase in the population of men serving sentences for offences of violence (including robbery) was not due to a *disproportionate* increase in receptions of men under sentence for those offences. In addition to an increase in the longest sentences, there was a shift in the distribution of sentence-lengths *under* five years for violent offences, toward the longer sentences; and this was reflected in an

[1] I am grateful to Mr R. T. Tudor, of the Home Office Statistical Division, for supplying these figures. For a further description of the estimates, see Appendix C below, pp. 132–135.

increasing concentration of men under sentence for violent offences in the prison population serving medium-term sentences. By contrast, sentences for housebreaking did not, in general, become longer; the increase in receptions in 1960–67 was greatest for those sentenced to one year or less. It seems likely that the association between violence and long sentences, and the consequent concentration of violent offenders among long-sentence prisoners, will increase in the future. The sentencing policies of the higher courts are unlikely to change in this respect in the near future; and if anything, as we shall see[1] the position has been aggravated by the measures introduced by the Criminal Justice Act 1967. Before discussing these changes, however, we must consider the way in which the prison population is distributed in the different types of institution which make up the English prison system.

The populations of different types of prison

The types of prison in the English prison system, and the general principles according to which different types of prisoners are allocated to these prisons, were described in Chapter II. In addition, we now have estimates of the numbers of prisoners in the population, who are serving sentences of different lengths for crimes of different types. This information does not make possible an exact description of the populations of different types of prison; but together with our Winson Green data, and published information from various other sources, we should be able to get at least a rough idea of this.

The population which we wish to distribute is the total population of about 22,000 males under sentence for criminal offences at the end of 1967. The proportions of this total population in different categories of institution—that is, general local prisons, special local, training and central prisons (both open and closed), and institutions for young prisoners and the mentally unstable—can be reckoned from the Prison Department's report for 1967,[2] provided we make an appropriate allowance for the small numbers of civil prisoners and of men on remand in the general and special local prisons. The Prison Department's report also gives a broad description of the types of men sent to each prison in 1967; it confirms, for example,

[1] Below, pp. 79–83.

[2] See RPD (1967), Appendix 3. This table gives the capacity, 1967 daily average and 1967 greatest population, for each prison in the system. I have used the daily average populations as the basis for my year-end estimates.

that open special local prisons (such as Drake Hall) received non-criminal, star and ordinary class prisoners serving short and medium sentences, and that Dartmoor received ordinary class prisoners serving long sentences. Information on the use of open prisons has been published from time to time in the Department's annual reports: for example, it has been noted that in certain open training prisons in recent years there have been experiments in mixing selected ordinary class prisoners in with the stars who form the majority of these institutions' populations.[1] Finally, we may take our data concerning the Winson Green population in 1966 as a basis for estimates of the population of the general local prisons, which constitute the biggest single sector in the prison system.

Using this information, I have been able to prepare Tables IV.1 and IV.2, which show the estimated numbers of males under sentence at the end of 1967 in the different types of institution, classified by length of sentence and by types of current offence. It hardly needs emphasizing that these are only estimates, and that at present there is no way of knowing how accurate they are. Especially in the conditions of overcrowding which now prevail in the closed prisons, allocation policies have to be modified from time to time; and the multi-functional nature of many prisons (e.g. those containing special wings for Category A prisoners) also complicates the accounting. The smallness of numbers in some categories is a further problem; it will be seen that I have generally rounded my estimates to the nearest hundred, and in the present state of knowledge it is clear that no greater degree of precision is possible. It is also unfortunately true that little can now be said about regional differences, or about the composition of different institutions' populations in respect of other parameters such as previous criminality and family background. Nor, without making use of more complicated methods of analysis, is it possible to see clearly just how different types of prisoner move through that system, and how the prisons are related to the penal system as a whole.[2]

Nonetheless, subject to those qualifications, I do not believe that my present estimates are unreasonable; they are consistent with all of the available evidence, including the probabilities of transfer and the proportions of sentence spent in Winson Green before transfer,

[1] See RPD (1962), p. 14; RPD (1963), pp. 15–16; above, pp. 11–12. The ratio of stars to ordinaries in these prisons—which include Sudbury and Ashwell, in the Midland region—is now apparently about three to one.

[2] See Appendix A, below, pp. 112–124.

Table IV.1

Estimated male populations of different types of English prisons at the end of 1967, by type of current offence

Type of Offence	*Type of Prison*										
	General Local	*Special Open*	*Local Closed*	*Training Open*	*Training Closed**	*Central Open*	*Central Closed*	*Total Open*	*Total Closed*	*Total All Prisons*	*Per cent of total*
Murder	20	—	—	—	—	—	420	—	440	440	2·0
Other violence against the person	1,180	—	320	70	400	—	600	70	2,500	2,570	11·6
Indictable sexual offences†	510	—	140	—	460	—	340	—	1,450	1,450	6·5
Breaking offences	4,060	290	270	900	900	245	345	1,435	5,575	7,010	31·7
Larceny	3,775	350	480	490	420	85	80	925	4,755	5,680	25·7
Fraud, False pretences	535	150	50	250	130	55	10	455	725	1,180	5·3
Other indictable (including robbery)	680	15	20	45	450	10	300	70	1,450	1,520	6·9
Other offences	1,480	545	170	45	40	5	5	595	1,695	2,290	10·3
Total	12,240	1,350	1,450	1,800	2,800	400	2,100	3,550	18,590	22,140	100·0

* Includes Northallerton and Aylesbury (YPs) and Grendon Underwood.
† Both homosexual and heterosexual.

Table IV.2

Estimated male populations of different types of English prisons at the end of 1967, by length of sentence

Length of Sentence	*General Local*	*Special Local*		*Training*		*Central*		*Total*		*Total, All Prisons*	*Per cent of total*
		Open	*Closed*	*Open*	*Closed**	*Open*	*Closed*	*Open*	*Closed*		
Up to 1 month	280	—	—	—	—	—	—	—	280	280	1·3
1 month up to 3 months	1,400	310	150	—	—	—	—	310	1,550	1,860	8·4
3 months up to 6 months	2,210	600	520	—	—	—	—	600	2,730	3,330	15·0
6 months up to 1 year	2,400	360	480	10	60	—	—	370	2,940	3,310	15·0
1 year up to 2 years	3,400	80	300	740	930	—	—	820	4,630	5,450	24·6
2 years up to 3 years	1,720	—	—	640	880	—	—	640	2,600	3,240	14·6
3 years up to 4 years	430	—	—	220	550	90	100	310	1,080	1,390	6·3
4 years up to 5 years	240	—	—	190	360	50	290	240	890	1,130	5·1
5 years up to 7 years	80	—	—	—	20	180	600	180	700	880	4·0
7 years up to 10 years	40	—	—	—	—	60	390	60	430	490	2·2
Over 10 years	40	—	—	—	—	20	720	20	760	780	3·5
Total	12,240	1,350	1,450	1,800	2,800	400	2,100	3,550	18,590	22,140	100·0

* Includes Northallerton and Aylesbury (YPs) and Grendon Underwood.

for our 1963 and 1966 samples.[1] Given a system of institutions which works in even approximately the way that the English prison system is known to work, Tables 5 and 6 seem to me to present the kinds of balance-sheets which one would expect that system to have had, at the end of 1967.

Implications for the operation of the system

It is also important to see that if the estimates in Tables IV.1 and IV.2 are even approximately correct, the implications for the operation of the prison system, and the treatment of prisoners, are considerable. For one thing, it might be thought that the marked differences in the inputs and populations of different types of institutions would lead to some corresponding differences in those institutions' regimes. The closed central prisons, for example, which take those serving the longest sentences, contain very high proportions of men convicted of violence against the person, robbery and serious sexual offences: the same is true, though to a lesser degree, of closed special local prisons whose populations consist largely of star prisoners thought unsuitable for open conditions. The open prisons, by contrast, contain almost exclusively property offenders: men who (in most cases) have no past history of criminal violence of any kind. The closed training prisons are in an intermediate position.

On this ground alone, it can be argued that the regimes of these types of institution should differ. The nature of violent personal crime and sexual offences differs markedly from that of non-violent acquisitive crime; and in the absence of contrary evidence, it seems reasonable to suppose that efforts at 'reform' should be different in each case. I am not suggesting, of course, that there are no differences between violent and sexual offenders, or that 'situational' murderers require the same treatment as, say, armed robbers (whose violence is largely instrumental) or rapists (whose violence may often be pathological). But the differences between these different types of 'personal' offender are, *prima facie*, much less marked than the differences between 'personal' offenders as a group, and the majority

[1] See above, pp. 49–52. Banks (*op. cit.*, pp. 13–14) presents some data on the Parkhurst population in March 1967, which show that 44 per cent of that central prison's population were then serving sentences for offences of violence (including robbery) or sexual offences. Dr Banks notes that this percentage is not as large as one would expect, because the prison had recently received on bulk transfer a largish group of men serving sentences of less than five years.

of thieves and burglars.[1] Moreover, the segregation of these two groups into different types of institution is a consequence of the present operation of the English prison system, even if it is not an intended consequence. There seems no good reason why it should not be taken into account in the institutions' respective regimes.

In fact, so far as I can discover, this does not at present happen. There are, of course, differences in the regimes of open prisons, 'progressive' training prisons and 'traditional' closed central prisons. But these differences are due to other considerations—of which security is among the most obvious—and are not, except accidentally, related to the nature of the inmates' criminality. There seem to be two reasons for this. The first is that very often—perhaps in the great majority of cases—prison staff do not know any more than broad legal descriptions of the prisoners' current and previous crimes; often (with the exception of the governor and one or two others) they may not even know this much. In a busy and overcrowded general local prison, with a high proportion of short-sentence prisoners, this is perhaps understandable—especially in view of the present abysmal state of records relating to these prisoners.[2] In other types of prison, however, the situation is in my experience often the same, since there appear to be no generally recognized channels through which detailed information about the prisoners' criminality is disseminated to the landing officers, workshop instructors and others who have to deal with the prisoners throughout their time in the institutions. Of course, the prisoner's current offence (and possibly his past history) will be noted if it raises any question of security: if, for example, he is likely to have associates who will try to help him escape, or if he has killed or molested a child and thus needs protection from his fellow-prisoners. But apart from this, the social context of the prisoner's criminal behaviour, its apparent motivation, his relations with other criminals and the development of his criminal career all seem to receive little attention in the planning of institutional regimes and individual prisoner's treatment, simply because little is known about them.

The second reason for this is really an argument, to the effect that exactly what the prisoner has done 'on the outside' is *irrelevant* to

[1] For a good discussion of this problem see Don C. Gibbons, *Changing the Lawbreaker* (Englewood Cliffs, N.J.: Prentice-Hall, 1965), esp. pp. 135–141.

[2] There has recently been a considerable improvement in these records where men serving longer sentences are concerned, owing to the introduction of parole. See further below, pp. 128–129.

his treatment in prison. What the prison staff must deal with (the argument runs) is the man himself, as he is now, in the institution; not an act which he did on one occasion some time previously. This is, of course, a variant of a familiar general theme concerning the 'treatment' of offenders at the present day: 'individualization' may apply where the man's personal welfare and psychological problems are concerned, but may (or even should) be avoided when the behaviour which got him into prison in the first place is being considered. It must be admitted that there is at present no hard empirical evidence that different reformative methods are required for, e.g., the man who repeatedly fails to control his tendency to use physical violence in public-house brawls, and the opportunistic, non-violent housebreaker or thief. Nonetheless, since the avowed purpose of the prison system is to stop its inmates from committing crimes, it would seem reasonable to experiment with different regimes deliberately related to different types of criminality, in those institutions whose populations (relatively homogeneous in themselves) differ markedly from one another in this respect. It might prove profitable, in other words, to capitalize on this consequence of the system's operation, rather than ignoring it as now seems the general rule.

Another important consequence of the present operation of the prison system is that the most promising treatment resources of the system—the open prisons, and the closed training prisons—are largely expended on those inmates who have the least need for them; that is, star prisoners and the less criminal ordinaries. This is, by itself, a penological commonplace: no doubt it is an inevitable result of the conflict which must exist between the competing objectives of security and reform.[1] It is indeed possible that a more liberal use of open (and closed training) prisons for recidivists might lead to a lower overall rate of reconviction; the recent experiments, already mentioned, of mixing star and ordinary prisoners in open institutions like Ashwell are a promising first step in this direction, though as experiments they still remain to be evaluated. But in the absence of further evidence on the relative effectiveness of open prisons (and closed training prisons), perhaps not too much weight should be put on this point. What is of more interest is the relationship between the formal goals and regimes of the different types of English prison

[1] Something similar apparently happened, for example, in the borstal system in the post-war period: see Roger Hood, *Borstal Reassessed* (London: Heinemann, 1965), p.158.

—in particular, the differing emphasis placed on security—and the resulting attitudes and values of the inmates in those institutions. Several American studies have found marked differences in the expressed attitudes and values of inmates in 'treatment-oriented' and 'custody-oriented' prisons: those in the former type were found to have much more favourable attitudes to prison staff, treatment programmes, etc., and to display different patterns of attitude change during their sentences.[1] Unfortunately it is somewhat difficult, in most of these studies, to separate the effects of differences in the formal goals of the institutions from differences in their inputs, since in general the less criminal inmates were sent to the less 'custody-oriented' institutions. But this is not invariably true, in the English prison system: a substantial minority of men serving long sentences for sexual or violent offences (who are thus likely to be sent to closed institutions like Dartmoor or Parkhurst, and in particular to Wakefield) have little or no previous prison experience.

It will also be seen from Table IV.2 (above, p. 64) that there are marked differences between different types of prison in population 'turnover'—that is, the rate at which the population changes as some men are discharged or transferred out, and others transferred in to replace them. In the closed central prisons, even making allowance for time spent in local prisons at the beginning (and possibly the end) of sentences, the average effective length of sentence must be of the order of four to five years. Thus, on average, about 20–25 per cent of the population will change in any one year; a man transferred into such a prison will have continuous contact, for two or three years, with much the same group of fellow-inmates. Since he will probably also have a good deal in common with many of those men, and since conditions in the uncrowded closed central prisons make possible a fair amount of association between prisoners, it is likely that he will enter into significant social relationships with at least some of his fellow-inmates. It is in these conditions that we should expect an inmate social system, informal social stratification, leadership roles, group norms and the like to develop among prisoners. At

[1] See B. B. Berk, 'Organizational Goals and Inmate Organization', (1966) 71 *Am. J. Sociol.* 522; O. Grusky, 'Organizational Goals and the Behaviour of Informal Leaders', (1959) 65 *Am. J. Sociol.* 59; David Street, R. D. Vinter, and Charles Perrow, *Organization for Treatment* (New York: Free Press, 1966), chap. 6; David Street, 'The Inmate Group in Custodial and Treatment Settings' (1965), 30 *Am. Sociol. Rev.* 40. For a general discussion of the problem see Thomas Mathiesen, 'The Sociology of Prisons: problems for future research', (1966) 17 *Brit. J. Sociol.* 360, esp. pp. 363–367.

the other extreme, in the general and special local prisons, the population turnover is much higher; as we have seen,[1] the average time spent in Winson Green by our 1966 receptions sample was only 50 days, though this average concealed some wide variations. Here we should expect relationships between inmates to be minimal, especially in view of the present overcrowded conditions. Again, the training prisons are in an intermediate category, with no overcrowding but with average effective sentences of only about a year; however, it is probable that there are marked differences between different institutions in this category, owing to other differences in their inputs.[2]

Inter-institutional differences in length of sentence and type of current offence are also relevant to the organization of prison welfare and after-care. Inmates sent to training and central prisons, often far from their homes, may need extensive 'transitional' measures (hostels, working-out schemes, home visits, etc.) both before and after they are released. Inmates in general local prisons, however, have very different problems; it is easier for them to maintain ties with their home communities, and the shorter time which they spend in prison means there is less need to worry about reintegrating them into those communities. In their case, prison welfare and after-care might well be regarded as part of a continuous programme of treatment in the community—especially since a number of them, as we have seen, tend to enter the same prison fairly often, for short periods of time. For example, group counselling programmes started in the prison might be extended to the local community after discharge.[3] In recent years, of course, local prisons have played a larger part in the pre-release treatment of long-sentence prisoners, through such things as prison hostel schemes. Nonetheless, the problems of the long-sentence prisons and the predominantly short-sentence ones are clearly different so far as welfare and after-care are concerned.[4]

[1] See above, pp. 45–46.

[2] For some American evidence bearing on this point, see Daniel Glaser, *The Effectiveness of a Prison and Parole System*, *op. cit.*, pp. 96–98.

[3] One such experiment was in fact carried out by the psychologist at Winson Green, though it was not, apparently, a conspicuous success. See P. Shapland. 'short-sentence recidivist groups and after-care', (1966) 5 *Prison Service Journal* 40. For a discussion of the work of welfare officers in English prisons, and its impact on offenders, see J. P. Martin and D. Webster, *The Social Consequences of Conviction* (London: Heinemann, 1971) Chap. 7, esp. pp. 153–157.

[4] Another factor suggested by our Winson Green data (above chapter III) must also be taken into account. This is that general local prisons are likely to contain a larger proportion of unmarried and generally socially isolated men

A further and potentially serious consequence of the system's present concentration of long-sentence violent offenders is the problem of security which these men present. Only a minority of this group, of course, will be in security Category A (maximum security); but the fact that they constitute such a large fraction of the population in a few prisons must be a cause of concern from the point of view of the prison staff if not the general public. The question whether Category A prisoners should be concentrated in one prison (as recommended by Lord Mountbatten[1]) was further considered by a Subcommittee of the Advisory Council on the Penal System, which recommended instead that these prisoners should be dispersed into four institutions.[2] But the issue of 'concentration' or 'dispersal' has not been considered in relation to violent men who are *not* classified as maximum-security prisoners (as the majority are not). Yet as the recent disturbances in Parkhurst prison show,[3] this group can undoubtedly create problems of containment for the staff, which might be reduced if their numbers in any single institution (such as Parkhurst) were not so great.

---

than training prisons or (in particular) open institutions. Again, this is clearly an unintended consequence of the operation of the system; but it seems a clearly unsatisfactory one, from the point of view of maintaining family and community relationships among those prisoners who have them. However, the position may be better at some other prisons (in particular, the smaller ones): cf. J. P. Martin and D. Webster, *The Social Consequences of Conviction* (London: Heinemann, 1971), Chap IV, esp. pp. 77–83.

[1] Report of the Inquiry into Prison Escapes and Security, Cmnd. 3175 of 1966 (London: HMSO), paras 212–216.

[2] Advisory Council on the Penal System, *The Regime for Long-term Prisoners in Conditions of Maximum Security* (London: HMSO, 1967), section iv.

[3] See *The Times*, 24 October 1969.

V

Recent Changes in the System

Having sketched the structure of the English prison system, I wish now to consider some problems which may arise when changes are made in such a system, or in other aspects of the penal system of which it is a part. Given that there are connections of the kind described in earlier chapters, between different penal measures, it should be obvious that changes in one part of the system—for example, the introduction of a new form of sentence, or a change in allocation policies—may affect other parts of the system. Yet too often, in recent years, this fact seems to have received little attention when questions of penal reform have been discussed and new legislation introduced.

The problems which may arise as a result of such changes are not by any means peculiar to prisons, nor to the English penal system. For example, the introduction of detention centres for offenders under 21 has undoubtedly led to a change in the input of the borstal system in the past few years;[1] many of the less criminally sophisticated adolescent offenders, of a kind who would formerly have been sent to borstal, were sent to detention centres instead, with the result that the 'quality' of borstal receptions has declined in comparison with earlier years.[2] The borstals' input must have been further affected by the changes in sentencing policy introduced by s. 3 of the Criminal Justice Act 1961, which in effect made borstal the standard medium-term sentence for offenders under 21, rather than a measure for offenders thought suitable for special training or treatment.[3] Each

[1] Detention centres were introduced by s. 18 of the Criminal Justice Act 1948; however, there were only two such centres until 1961. In 1968, about 40 per cent of boys committed to borstal training had previously been in detention centres.

[2] See the discussion in Roger Hood, *Borstal Reassessed* (London: Heinemann, 1965), chap. III, esp. pp. 83–89; Alan Little, 'Borstal Success and the Quality of Borstal Inmates', (1962) 2 *Brit. J. Criminol.* 271. As Little's article makes clear, the 'quality' of the borstal input—as measured by the Mannheim-Wilkins prediction table—was declining even before the use of detention centres became substantial.

[3] The interpretation of this statute by the Court of Criminal Appeal, and its implications, are discussed in J. E. Hall Williams and D. A. Thomas, 'The Use of Imprisonment and Borstal Training for Young Offenders under the Criminal Justice Act 1961' [1965], *Crim. L.R.* 146, 193, 273.

of these changes may have been well justified, in terms of the overall cost-effectiveness of the penal system; but each must have led to considerable changes in the regimes and conditions of borstal training, which might have been more effectively carried out if they had been more fully anticipated.[1]

Changes in the lengths of sentences may also have marked effects on the populations of penal institutions. For example, in the United States, the mandatory minimum prison sentences provided by Federal law for certain narcotics offences were raised in 1956 to five years for a first offence and ten years for second and subsequent offences.[2] The effects of this change on the population of the Federal prison system appears to have been considerable: in 1951 drug-law violators constituted about 11 per cent of the total prison population, whereas in 1965 they made up about 18 per cent, even though receptions into prison for narcotics offences did not substantially increase during that period.[3]

In England, a similar situation occurred with the introduction, in 1948, of the special sentences of corrective training and preventive detention. These measures were intended to provide longer sentences than would be justified as punishment, for special classes of persistent offenders. In the case of corrective training the sentence could be of two, three or four years, subject to the normal rules concerning remission; in practice, three years was the commonest length until 1962, when two-year sentences became the general rule.[4] In the case of preventive detention, the sentence might be from five to fourteen years; seven years was, in practice, the most usual. Originally, though preventive detainees might receive one-third remission of sentence, the majority were allowed only one-sixth; but in 1963, following a report of the Advisory Council on the Treatment of Offenders, one-

[1] The reports of the Prison Department in recent years contain many references to the poor 'quality' of borstal receptions: see, e.g., RPC (1962), chap. 4; RPD (1963), chap. 4. On the other factors leading to changes in the borstal regime in this period see Hood, *op. cit.*, 74–82.

[2] The offences are those of unlawful sale or importation. Suspension of sentence, probation and parole are prohibited for all but first offences of unlawful possession: see the Internal Revenue Code of 1964, 26 USC s. 7237.

[3] See the President's Commission on Law Enforcement and Administration of Justice, Task Force on Narcotics and Drug Abuse (Washington, DC: US Government Printing Office, 1967), pp. 11–12; exact figures are given in the Federal Prisoner Statistics for 1966, p. 16.

[4] For a review of sentencing policy and practice concerning corrective training, see J. D. McLean, 'Corrective Training—Decline and Fall' [1964] *Criminal L.R.* 745; and A. E. Bottoms, 'Towards a Custodial Training Sentence for Adults' [1965] *Crim. L.R.*, 582.

third remission was granted in all cases.[1] Both corrective training and preventive detention were abolished by s. 37 of the Criminal Justice Act 1967. Preventive detention was replaced by a similar measure known as the extended sentence;[2] but this measure has so far been very little used, there being only 30 such receptons in 1968.

The populations of men serving sentences of corrective training and preventive detention can be estimated in the same way as for ordinary imprisonment, since these sentences were also for fixed terms. For most years, in fact, exact figures for the total year-end populations in these groups were published in the annual reports of the Prison Department. These populations, and total annual receptions under each form of sentence, are shown in Figure 3. It will be

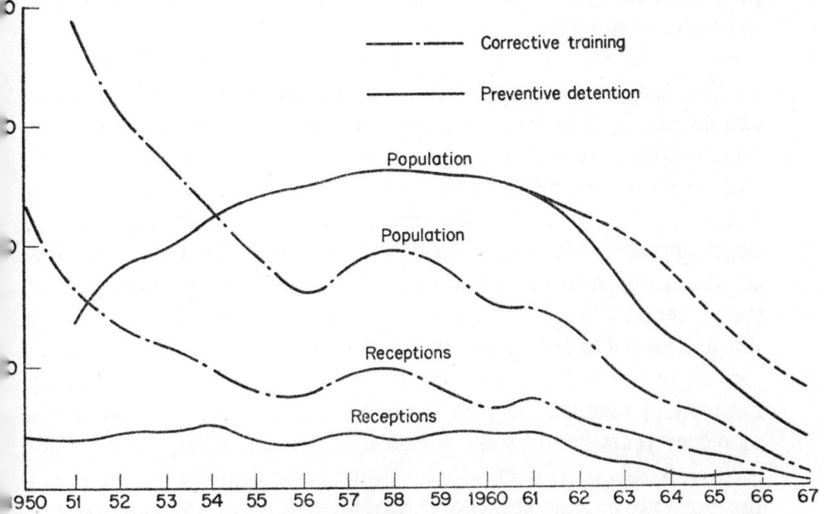

Figure 3. Receptions and year end populations (males), preventive detention and corrective training, 1950–1967.

seen from this graph that the population of corrective trainees, with average effective sentence lengths of between 1·33 and 2·0 years, is fairly responsive to changes in the annual numbers of receptions. But the population of preventive detainees—with effective lengths of sentence ranging from about 5·0 years up to about 11·6 years—changes much less quickly, since a smaller fraction of that population

[1] See the report of the Advisory Council on the Treatment of Offenders. *Preventive Detention* (London: HMSO, 1963), esp. pp. 12–15; and W. H. Hammond and E. Chayen, *Persistent Criminals* (London: HMSO, 1963), esp. chaps. 11, 16.

[2] Criminal Justice Act 1967, s. 39.

enters and leaves the system each year. (The decline in the preventive detention population from 1963 onwards is due mainly to the change in that year in policy concerning remission, which resulted in the early release of some 200 men.[1]) Only 170 preventive detainees were received into prison in the five years 1963–67; yet at the end of 1967 there were still 194 men in prison under this form of sentence, and if remission policy had not been changed the number would probably have been about 350.

To some extent, combining the populations of preventive detainees and corrective trainees with the population serving sentences of ordinary imprisonment minimizes the increase, described in the last chapter, in the long-sentence population in the years since 1960. In fact, there must have been about 275 men serving long sentences of preventive detention (of ten years or over) at the end of 1960; their numbers declined in subsequent years, as the numbers of men serving long sentences of ordinary imprisonment were rising. It should not be thought, however, that these changes in input completely offset one another, and so placed no strain on the system: since the *types* of prisoner in the two groups of long-sentence men were very different. The majority of men sentenced to preventive detention were relatively petty thieves and housebreakers, very few of whom had records of violence; a substantial proportion were of the inadequate 'habitual prisoner' type described by West,[2] who were not dangerous to the public and posed virtually no security problem for the prison system. By contrast, as has already been noted, the majority of men receiving long sentences of ordinary imprisonment in recent years have been convicted of murder, robbery and other serious crimes of violence. As a group, these men are younger than the preventive detainees, more aggressive, less socially isolated and maladapted, and certainly more dangerous both to the prison system and the general public. The consequences of this change in input, for the few institutions containing both types of prisoner, must have been considerable.[3]

A further general point about the structure of the prison population, and the relation between receptions and population, should be noted. As we have seen, the input to the English prison system con-

[1] See RPD (1962), pp. 13–14.

[2] See D. J. West, *The Habitual Prisoner* (London: Macmillan, 1963), esp. chap. 4; and Hammond and Chayen, *op. cit.*, chap. 6.

[3] Some data on this point, relating to Blundeston prison, are presented in Banks, 'Prison Receptions and Population', *op. cit.*, pp. 12–14.

sists of a large number of men serving fairly short sentences, and much smaller numbers committed for long periods: thus there is a high negative correlation between numbers received and effective time spent in the system. For this reason, it seems clear that at the present time it should be easier to reduce the size of the system's population by reducing the effective lengths of the longer sentences, than by trying to reduce the numbers received under short sentences. No doubt there is little scope for reducing the very longest sentences now imposed by the higher courts (those of, say, over ten years), owing to current judicial attitudes to deterrence and the protection of the public; there are, in any case, very few such sentences in any year. At the other extreme, while it might in theory be desirable to find alternative ways of dealing with those given short prison sentences (of, say, six months or less), this may well be difficult to accomplish, given the existing sentencing practices of the courts.[1] Yet unless receptions under short sentences are very substantially reduced, the effect on the prison population will be negligible. For these reasons, if it is desired to reduce the total prison population, the group of men serving medium-to-long term sentences—of, say, over three years and up to ten years—would seem to be those most easily removed from the system. For example, a 20 per cent reduction in the average effective lengths of this group's sentences would, in recent years, have reduced the prison population by about 1,300 men; in 1967 this would have entailed (at worst) reducing the sentences passed on about 2,000–2,500 offenders a year, which would certainly not have been impossible for the higher courts to achieve by a moderate adjustment of sentencing 'tariffs'. To obtain the same reduction in the prison population by cutting the numbers received for short periods—say, six months or less—would have been much more difficult, and perhaps impossible. In 1967 there were nearly 33,000 receptions under sentences of these lengths, two-thirds of which were for three months or less; yet because of the shortness of their effective sentences these men's *total* contribution to the average prison population at the end of 1967 was less than 6,000 in all.

It is for this reason that, in my opinion, the parole system introduced in 1968[2] holds the best chance of reducing the prison system's population. So far, however, parole has made only a limited impact

[1] See above, chap. II, pp. 20–23; and below, pp. 92–94.
[2] Criminal Justice Act 1967, ss. 59–64.

on the prison population. The Parole Board's first report reveals that of the 4,764 prisoners (male and female) eligible for parole on 1 April 1968, only 406 (or 8·5 per cent) were finally recommended for release, some of whom would shortly have been released in any case. Of the prisoners becoming eligible between 1 April and 31 December 1968 a total of 594, or 14 per cent, were recommended for parole on first review, and a further 157 on second review. The release rate was higher in 1969: of the 7,278 cases eligible in that year, 1,835 (or 25·2 per cent) were released on either first or second review.[1] But since these prisoners' periods on licence have often been fairly short —in half of the 1969 cases it was less than six months—the extent to which parole has reduced the prison population to date can hardly be called substantial.[2] I am not suggesting, of course, that the only (or even the most important) function of parole should be to reduce the numbers of men in prison. But given the present pressure of numbers in the English prison system, it is surely absurd to ignore the possibility of using release on parole to reduce the numbers in custody, especially in view of the utter lack of evidence to date that parole has any other penological advantages.

Other effects of the Criminal Justice Act 1967

The Criminal Justice Act 1967 made two other important changes in the English penal system, which were intended to reduce the number of offenders committed to prison. First, new methods of enforcing the payment of fines were provided, and the powers of the courts to imprison offenders for non-payment of fines were correspondingly reduced. Secondly, the courts were required to suspend prison sentences in certain cases, and were given a discretionary power to suspend them in others. These measures did not come into force until the beginning of 1968, so it is not yet possible to make a full assessment of their effects on the prison system; indeed, it may be some time before the full consequences of these changes can be evaluated. However, some evidence concerning the early effects of the two innovations is available, and will be summarized here.

[1] See the Report of the Parole Board for 1968, House of Commons paper No. 290, 17 June 1969 (London: HMSO), Appendices 1 and 2; Report for 1969, House of Commons paper No. 48, 14 July 1970, Appendix 1.

[2] According to the 1969 Report, the *average* time on licence for the 1969 releases was 'about seven months'; the average effective sentences of these men (allowing for remission) was about 3½ years.

The enforcement of fines

By s. 44 of the Act, magistrates' courts are in general prohibited from imprisoning any offender for non-payment of a fine, and from fixing an alternative term of imprisonment for non-payment, on the occasion of convicting him; they must enquire on at least one subsequent occasion into the offender's means to pay, and may not imprison in default unless all other methods of enforcing payment appear to be 'inappropriate or unsuccessful'. Section 47 contains similar provisions relating to the higher courts. Other sections empower the courts to make attachment of earnings orders concerning fine-defaulters,[1] and to enforce payment of fines in the High Court or county court;[2] the Act also increased the maximum fines for a wide range of offences,[3] and reduced slightly the maximum periods of imprisonment for non-payment of fines.[4]

Receptions of fine-defaulters into prison fell by almost exactly a third in 1968, compared with the preceding year. Among adult males, who account for the majority of fine-defaulters, the reduction in committals was greatest for those not given time to pay; as a result, nearly three-fourths of those committed to prison in default in 1968 had had some time to pay. But there was very little change in the previous recorded criminality or prison experience of fine-defaulters, about 40 per cent of whom apparently had not been in prison before. The decrease in receptions in default is due in part, however, to a drop in the numbers of offenders fined by the courts (and so at risk of defaulting on payment) in 1968. Moreover, the changes introduced by the 1967 Act have lengthened the fine-enforcement process, and will thus have produced a time-lag in receptions into prison in default; thus for some offenders committal to prison will merely have been postponed, not prevented. In any case, as we have seen, the contribution of fine-defaulters to the prison population is a small one, owing to the short periods of time which they tend to spend in prison; the maximum reduction in the system's population to be expected from these measures is thus likely to be of the order of 300–400 men. Bearing in mind the characteristics of our Winson Green defaulters,[5] it seems highly optimistic to expect this maximum.

[1] s. 46 and Schedule 1; and see the Maintenance Orders Act 1958.
[2] s. 45.
[3] ss. 43, 92 and Schedule 3; see also s. 91 concerning fines for drunkenness.
[4] s. 93.
[5] See above, pp. 30–34. Results of a more detailed study of fine-defaulters in Birmingham, which we carried out concurrently with the present research, will be

The suspended sentence

Section 39 of the 1967 Act provides that any court which passes a sentence of imprisonment of six months or less (in respect of one offence) *must* suspend that sentence, unless the offence involves an assault or the threat of violence, the possession of a firearm or offensive weapon, or indecency with a child or young person; or it is one for which the offender was placed on probation or conditionally discharged; or unless the offender has already served a prison or borstal sentence, or been subject to a suspended sentence.[1] This section also provides that a court which passes a prison sentence of two years or less *may* suspend that sentence, regardless of the type of offence or the offender's antecedents. The period of suspension, for both mandatory and discretionary suspended sentences, may be from one to three years. If the offender is convicted during this period of a further offence punishable by imprisonment, then by s. 40 the court dealing with him on that occasion may—and normally shall—order that the suspended sentence shall take effect with the original term unaltered; it may, however, order a shorter term of imprisonment, or extend the period of suspension, or make no order at all.

In *R v. Ithell*[2] the Court of Appeal held that the proper approach, where a fresh offence is committed during a period of suspension, is for the court first to sentence the offender for the fresh offence, and thereafter address itself to the question of the suspended sentence. The facts of the subsequent offence are clearly relevant to the decision whether to implement a suspended sentence: and each case must be considered in the light of its own facts.[3] It has been held, for example,

---

published elsewhere. In addition, an evaluative study of the changes in the enforcement of fines made by the 1967 Act is being carried out by the Home Office.

[1] Or, of course, if he is being sent to prison immediately for another offence for which suspension is not required. If consecutive sentences totalling more than two years are passed, the power to suspend does not arise: *R* v. *Coleman* [1969] 2 All E.R. 1074. But if a case falls within the mandatory requirement, and if the court wishes to sentence the offender to six months on each of two counts, it must suspend both sentences even if they are consecutive: *R* v. *Flanders* [1968] 3 All E.R. 534 [1969], 1 Q.B. 148. In an unreported case, however, (*R* v *Brown.*, 26 July 1968; see [1968] 3 All E.R. 536 n.) the Court of Appeal noted that this difficulty only arises if two consecutive sentences are given, and can be avoided by two one-year concurrent terms! See also *R* v. *March* [1970] 2 All E.R. 536.

[2] [1969] 2 All E.R. 449.

[3] *R* v. *Griffiths* [1969] 2 All E.R. 805, (1969) 53 Cr. App. R.424: in this case a suspended sentence for housebreaking was implemented, on a man with many previous convictions for housebreaking and violence, on his subsequent convic-

that a court may properly consider it 'unjust'[1] to activate a suspended sentence where the new offence is comparatively trivial, and particularly where it is in a different category from the earlier offence.[2] But the normal course of events, when an offender is reconvicted after receiving a suspended sentence, is for that sentence to be imposed in full: this happened in about 88 per cent of the cases in which there were subsequent proceedings in 1968 and 1969 following a suspended sentence.[3] And in *R* v. *Ithell* the Court of Appeal also said that 'unless there are some quite exceptional circumstances, the suspended sentence should be ordered to run consecutive to the sentence for the subsequent offence.'[4]

At first sight this measure seems to hold considerable promise of reducing the prison population; there were about 1,500 men received into prison in 1967 who were apparently within the scope of the mandatory suspended sentence, and nearly 28,000 to whom the discretionary sentence could have been applied. However, in the light of our preceding discussion, two things about this measure stand out clearly. The first is that its impact on the prison *population* is less than appears, because it is aimed primarily at reducing receptions under the shorter sentences of imprisonment. Since the effective length of a six-month sentence is of the order of 0·35 of a year, three such sentences must be prevented in order to reduce the average population by one man.

A much more serious limitation of the suspended sentence can be seen by reflecting upon the criteria of eligibility for the mandatory variety of it. Broadly speaking, this measure is aimed at offenders against property, who have not previously been in prison or borstal; and given the nature of judicial sentencing policies, it is clear that it is also this type of offender who is most likely to be dealt with by means of the discretionary suspended sentence. But as

---

tion for dangerous driving and assaulting a police constable. See also *R v. Dutton* [1969] *Crim. L.R.* 612.

[1] Criminal Justice Act 1967, s. 40 (1).

[2] *R v. Moylan* [1969] 3 All E.R. 783; cf. *R* v. *Ford* [1969] 3 All E.R. 782; *R* v. *Williams* [1969] *Crim. L.R.* 669. See also *R* v. *Preece* [1970] *Crim. L.R.* 296, where the triviality of the subsequent offence was approved as a ground for implementing a suspended sentence with its length reduced.

[3] See Table IX of the Criminal Statistics for 1968, Cmnd, 4098, p. 211; and for 1969, Cmnd. 4398, p. 203.

[4] [1969] 2 All E.R. 449, at 450, per Edmund Davies J. (approving the statement of Ld Parker, CJ, in *R.* v. *Brown*, *The Times*, 12 November 1968). There are exceptions, however: e.g. if the subsequent sentence is an extended term (*R* v. *Wilkinson* [1969] 3 All E.R. 1263) or another suspended sentence (*R* v. *Blakeway* [1969] 3 All E.R. 1133).

we have seen, it is precisely these offenders who—as non-violent 'star' prisoners—were likely, before the 1967 Act, to be sent to *open* prisons. And as we have also seen, open prisons in England are not, and never have been, overcrowded. In other words, given the legal criteria of offenders deemed suitable for the suspended sentence, it could be predicted that this measure would be most likely to reduce overcrowding in a part of the English prison system in which overcrowding does not occur.

It seems clear that this was, in fact, precisely what happened in the first year in which the suspended sentence was available to the English courts. According to the official Criminal Statistics for 1968, a total of 32,002 suspended sentences were imposed in that year. The effect on the input to the prison system was substantial: receptions in 1968 of adult males under sentence without the option of a fine fell by 22 per cent, compared with the preceding year. As would be expected, the reduction was especially great among men with little previous criminality and prison experience. Receptions of men with no previous convictions fell by over half; and there were similar, though slightly smaller, decreases among those with one or two previous proved offences. Receptions of men with no previous prison experience also fell sharply—by about 45 per cent, compared with 1967. As a result, less than 5 per cent of the 'no option' receptions in 1968 were of men with no previous recorded convictions (compared with about 8 per cent in the preceding year); and only 20 per cent of those received in 1968 had no previous institutional experience, compared with 28 per cent in 1967. At the other extreme, there was little change in the numbers of recidivists received; thus 68 per cent had over five previous convictions in 1968, against 58 per cent in 1967.

In addition to a higher proportion of recidivists, the men received into prison in 1968 contained a higher proportion under sentence for the more serious types of offence than those received in 1967. There was an especially big drop in the numbers received under sentence for non-indictable, and akin to indictable, offences, and for aggravated forms of larceny. The proportion of receptions under sentence for violent and sexual crimes rose slightly, from 14 per cent in 1967 to over 17 per cent in 1968. Unfortunately, statistics of the lengths of suspended sentences imposed by the courts are not very detailed. But the drop in receptions into prison in that year was greatest, proportionately, for sentences of six months or less; the numbers received under sentences of three months or less fell by half, compared with 1967.

The average population of adult male prisoners fell to 20,965 in 1968, and by March 1969 it had dropped still further to 20,698 (including fine-defaulters).[1] Nonetheless, according to the Prison Department's report for 1968, 'the reduction was uneven and heavy pressure continued to be felt on local prison and remand centre accommodation'; moreover, an initial effect of the introduction of the suspended sentence (and parole) 'appears to have been a reduction in the numbers of prisoners suitable for open conditions'.[2] As can be seen from Table V.1, the average population of the general

Table V.1

Capacity and population of English prisons for males, 1967 and 1968

	Type of institution				
	General local	*Remand centres*	*Open*	*Other Closed*	*Total*
1967:					
Capacity	10,621	1,246	4,300	7,080	23,247
Average population	14,779	1,360	3,945	6,825	26,909
% of capacity	*139·1*	*109·1*	*91·7*	*96·4*	*115·8*
1968:					
Capacity	10,206	1,248	4,281	7,448	23,183
Average population	13,063	1,307	3,118	7,224	24,712
% of capacity	*128·0*	*104·7*	*72·8*	*97·0*	*106·6*
Change in average population, 1967–68:					
Number	−1,716	−53	−827	+399	−2,197
%	*−11·6*	*−3·9*	*−21·0*	*+5·8*	*−8·2*

local prisons in 1968 was 12 per cent lower than it had been in 1967; but this was still 28 per cent more than their capacity. The average population of the open prisons, by contrast, was only 73 per cent of capacity in 1968; in the preceding year it had been 87 per cent.

Unfortunately, official reports also make it clear that even this limited relief is likely to be temporary. There was a sharp rise in overall population of prison service establishments in 1969; within

[1] See Cmnd. 4214, p. 118. [2] RPD (1968), pp. 3–4.

the first seven months it had already reached 35,000 and was approaching the high levels of 1967. For two different, though related, reasons the position may be even worse in the future. First, though many of those given suspended sentences in 1968 had not previously been in prison or borstal, and a number must have been first offenders, it is likely that many—perhaps the majority—had one or more previous convictions. The great majority were thieves and housebreakers, with—in all probability—a fairly high risk of recidivism. According to the White Paper *People in Prison*, of the 32,002 offenders given suspended sentences in 1968, 4,222 were committed to custody after a subsequent conviction in that year.[1] But this figure yields a rate of committal to prison of over 13 per cent, after an average time at risk (allowing for time spent awaiting trial) of only about five months. This suggests that the rate of recidivism over two years at risk will be about 35–40 per cent, and may well be higher than 50 per cent over three years. Since—as we have seen—the normal course of events when these offenders are reconvicted is for the suspended sentence to be imposed in full, consecutive to the prison sentence which is likely to be passed on that occasion, the probability is that most of those reconvicted after a suspended sentence will go to prison for a longer period of time than they would have done otherwise. There also exists a possibility—hopefully it is no more than that—that some judges are imposing longer terms of imprisonment when these are suspended, than they would have done if the imprisonment had been immediate.[2]

The second reason for pessimism about the effect of the suspended sentence is the fact that in both 1968 and 1969 it was clearly used to some extent by the courts in place of fines and probation, rather than in lieu of imprisonment. It was said by the Court of Appeal (Criminal Division) in a case[3] in December 1968 that a suspended sentence should only be imposed when, having eliminated all other

[1] Cmnd. 4214, p. 17. In 1969, there were 32,169 suspended sentences, and 8,742 persons were committed to custody on activation of suspended sentences: RPD (1969), p. 10.

[2] As is said to have happened when the suspended sentence was introduced in Israel. See D. Reifen, 'New Ventures of Law Enforcement in Israel' (1967), 58 *J. Crim. Law, Crim. & P.S.* 70, at 72.

[3] *R* v. *O'Keefe* [1969] 1 All E.R. 426. The court also noted that it had found many cases where suspended sentences were being given 'as what one might call a "soft option", when the court is not quite certain what to do, and in particular . . . many cases when suspended sentences have been given when the proper order was a probation order' (ibid, at p. 427).

alternatives, the court decides that the case is one for imprisonment. 'The court must go through the process of eliminating other possible courses such as absolute discharge, conditional discharge, probation order, fines, and then say to itself: this is a case for imprisonment, and the final question is, it being a case for imprisonment, is immediate imprisonment required, or can I give a suspended sentence?'[1] The effect of this *dictum* on the sentencing practices of the courts remains to be seen; but it does not seem likely that it will be great. There is unfortunately little reason, at present, to think that the sentencing policies enunciated by the Court of Appeal have much effect on sentencing in magistrates' courts, where the majority of suspended sentences have so far been imposed; and in any event it may well prove difficult for sentencers to apply the decision-making rule just quoted, without further guidance. It is clear, however, that a very different policy concerning the suspended sentence was often followed, by both higher courts and magistrates' courts, in both 1968 and 1969.

Table V.2, which summarizes the sentences passed on males aged 21 and over convicted of indictable offences in 1967, 1968 and 1969, shows clearly the extent to which this must have happened.[2] It is clear from this table that about two-thirds of those given suspended sentences in 1968 and 1969, at both magistrates' courts and the higher courts, would have been dealt with by something other than imprisonment if the suspended sentence had not been available: it seems likely that about half would have been fined, and one-sixth put on probation. Even if this does not continue to happen, the net effect of the suspended sentence may well be to increase the prison population rather than reducing it. And if it does continue to happen, the suspended sentence could easily turn out to be the most counter-productive penal reform ever enacted.

The possible adverse consequences of this measure become even more serious in the light of existing allocation policies within the prison system. Even though the immediate effect of the introduction of suspended sentences has mainly been to reduce the numbers in open prisons, it could serve, indirectly, to reduce the pressure of

[1] Ibid., at p. 428.

[2] A similar situation occurred in Israel when the suspended sentence was introduced there in 1954; the higher courts appear to have used it in lieu of fines and recognizances, as well as in lieu of immediate imprisonment. See Leslie Sebba, 'Penal Reform and Court Practice' (1969), 21 *Scripta Hierosolymitana* 133, at 149.

Table V.2

Sentences passed on males aged 21 and over convicted of indictable offences, 1967–1969 (in percentages)

	1967	*1968*	*1969*
Assizes and Quarter Sessions:			
Discharge	4·8	3·2	3·7
Fine	20·1	11·0	12·0
Probation	13·5	9·1	8·2
Imprisonment (immediate)			
6 months or less	9·4	7·7	9·3
Over 6 months, up to 1 year	18·7	17·1	17·7
Over 1 year, up to 2 year	20·0	18·0	17·4
Over 2 year	12·0	11·1	10·2
Suspended sentence	—	21·1	20·1
Other	1·5	1·7	1·5
Total	100·0	100·0	100·0
Numbers sentenced	21,664	23,491	26,358
Magistrates' courts:			
Discharge	9·8	10·2	10·3
Fine	64·9	55·6	57·5
Probation	8·9	6·6	6·5
Imprisonment (immediate)			
1 month or less	1·2	0·8	0·9
Over 1 month, up to 2 month	0·9	0·4	0·4
Over 2 month, up to 3 month	5·3	3·2	3·6
Over 3 month, up to 6 month	8·6	5·6	5·2
Suspended sentence	—	17·1	15·1
Other*	0·6	0·6	0·6
Total	100·0	100·0	100·0
Numbers sentenced	86,056	91,672	107,611

* Not including offenders committed to Quarter Sessions for sentence, who are however included in the totals for the higher courts. Percentages given sentences of different lengths at the higher courts have been estimated (from sentence-lengths on *all* males sentences at Assizes and Quarter Sessions); however, the total percentages given immediate imprisonment are correct as shown.

numbers in the general local prisons, by making possible the transfer of more men from those prisons to open institutions. But in practice, such a change in transfer policies is unlikely, in view of the existing limitations on the use of open prisons and the official estimates of the numbers of prisoners deemed suitable for them.[1] It may well be

[1] See above, pp. 18–19. This problem may of course be overcome by judicious 'reclassification', illustrating the extent to which 'suitability' is a function of space available.

that, of those offenders who are reconvicted after having been given suspended sentences, a high proportion will be suitable for open prisons, according to present standards: if so, the empty places in those prisons will presumably be filled again in time. But if the numbers received into prison in the next few years are actually increased because of the suspended sentence—and this seems a very real possibility—then the result will be to increase the existing pressure on *closed* institutions, owing to the policy of not allowing overcrowding in open prisons. This situation will be further aggravated by the increase in the effective lengths of sentences which the suspended sentence is likely to cause.

Some questions for future research

It must be stressed that this assessment of the effects on the prison system of the Criminal Justice Act 1967 is only a provisional one. It will be some time before the various measures introduced by the Act can be properly evaluated; and a full assessment of the suspended sentence must take into account not only the relative effectiveness of this measure in reducing recidivism, but also any changes in the effectiveness of imprisonment which may occur as a result of changes in the input (and population) of the prisons. It is fair to point out, moreover, that a reduction of the prison population was not the only objective which the suspended sentence was intended to accomplish; in addition, it was thought to be a good way of keeping out of prison people who should not be sent there, especially for short periods of time.[1] But a reduction in the rising prison population was certainly *one* intended objective of this measure; and it is striking that no consideration whatever appears to have been given to the possibility that this objective might not

[1] Thus, for example, in the Committee stage of the Criminal Justice Bill in the House of Commons in 1967, the then Home Secretary, Mr Roy Jenkins, stressed that one of the main purposes of the Bill was to reduce the numbers of persons sent to prison, 'not primarily because of the strain under which our prison system is suffering at the present time but primarily because I believe that it is a great mistake to acclimatise people to prison whenever it is unnecessary to do so'. Mr Jenkins noted that the rising prison population was an additional reason for reducing the numbers sent to prison, but emphasized that 'it [the introduction of the suspended sentence] is not a question of administrative convenience. It happens that here administrative convenience marches alongside with what I believe to be a basically right approach'. See the House of Commons Official Report, Standing Committee A, Criminal Justice Bill (Eleventh sitting, Wednesday, 22nd February 1967), cols. 544–545; cf. the Report of the Fourteenth Sitting (7th March 1967), col. 734.

be accomplished, or that exactly the opposite effect would be produced.

A general conclusion which can be drawn from the matters discussed in this chapter is that the working of penal systems, and the probable consequences of changes in those systems, are subjects on which much more research needs to be done. There is no reason whatever to suppose that the kinds of problems raised by the Criminal Justice Act 1967 are peculiar to the English penal system; on the contrary, it is likely that these problems can only be fully understood by means of comparative studies of a number of penal and judicial systems. Such studies could be of value for administrative purposes; they could also make an important contribution to the sociology of law and legal institutions, and also to the sociology of organizations.

The first priority for future researchers in this field is surely to realize that a penal system *is* a system, and not just a collection of independent and unrelated activities. It follows that there is little value in assessing the 'effectiveness' (in any sense) of a single penal measure, without any consideration of the other measures to which it is related. Theoretically, a change in the policy of a single police force in respect of the cautioning of young offenders may lead to a change of some kind, a number of years later, in the long-term prison population: for the two things are not independent. But it is also important not to fall into the error of thinking that there is something rigidly 'deterministic' about the operation of the penal system (or indeed any similar human system), so that it *must* operate in a certain way. On the contrary, the very fact that the allocation of different types of offenders to different penal measures is so largely governed by more or less definite rules and policies means that it is controllable, at least within limits.[1] An important first step, then, is to try to discover exactly how controllable the penal system is, and how well or badly the existing controls work in practice: that is, to see how far the treatment (in the broadest sense) of officially known offenders is regulated by definite policies, established practices and predictable economic and social factors in the system's environment.

[1] Of course, no such human system is ever *absolutely* controllable: the best-laid plans of economists and other social engineers occasionally still go wrong, though perhaps less frequently than they used to. But the main conclusion to be drawn from a vast amount of sociological research on organizational behaviour is surely a reassurring one: *most* people, *most* of the time, do what they are supposed to do.

Several related questions then immediately suggest themselves. Exactly what are the mechanisms by which the system is controlled? To what extent do similar policies and practices operate in different parts of the penal system, and what are the consequences of this? For example, it seems a reasonable hypothesis that in both England and the United States, the police, courts and penal institutions all tend to differentiate between offenders partly by reference to common notions of past moral fault; and partly on the basis of perceived incorrigibility or dangerousness, i.e. on an estimate of probable future misbehaviour. Other factors are also relevant, of course, especially with juveniles; and it seems clear that these things, together with the assessment of future behaviour, are likely to be affected by the *information* about offenders which is available to the agents of the system.[1] Changes in the amount or quality of this information may thus have a considerable effect on the operation of the system.[2] Another topic to be investigated is the possibility of alternative means of controlling the operation of the various parts of the penal system: for example, using 'treatment tribunals' or other administrative agencies to allocate offenders to different measures, rather than courts. If the principles followed by such agencies are likely to be the same as those generally followed by the courts—as often seems, in practice, to be the case[3]—then the only

[1] There will of course usually be differences in the attitudes, policies, etc., of the courts, police, probation officers and other agents of the system: see, for example, Stanton Wheeler *et. al.*, 'Agents of Control: A Comparative Analysis', in S. Wheeler (ed), *Controlling Delinquents* (New York: Wiley, 1968) pp. 31–60, esp. 45–50. As this excellent study makes clear, the relations between agency members' expressed attitudes to delinquency and the ways in which they tend to deal with offenders are complex. Cf. A. Cicourel, *The Social Organization of Juvenile Justice* (New York: Wiley, 1968), chaps. 5–6.

[2] On the influence of social enquiry reports by probation officers to the courts, see above, p. 22; and for a general outline of a model of the sentencing process based partly on information flow, see R. G. Hood and R. F. Sparks, *Key Issues in Criminology* (London: Weidenfeld, 1970), chap. 5.

[3] Thus, for example, a survey of parole board members in California found that the majority regarded the protection of the public and release at the optimal time for success on parole to be very important goals; deterrence and retribution were rated as unimportant. A later study of California parole decisions, however, showed legal offence, and severity of offence, to be important predictors of time in prison before release. See D. M. Gottfredson and K. B. Ballard, Jnr, *Estimating Prison and Parole Terms under an Undeterminate Sentence Law* (Institute for the Study of Crime and Delinquency, report No. 5, Vacaville, Calif.: 1964); and idem, *The Parole Decision: Some Agreements and Disagreements*, report No. 4 of the same Institute (1964). Cf. Paul Tappan, *Crime, Justice and Correction* (1960), pp. 461–462, on the reduction in disparity of prison terms following the creation of the California Adult Authority; for discussions of a similar situation in Sweden see the remarks of I. Strahl at the 6th Int. Congress of the Association du Droit Penal in Rome, 1953: *Comptes Rendues* (1957) at p. 237.

effect of such a change may be the reduction of disparity of treatment; even this may be minimal. A related question concerns the means of controlling judicial or quasi-judicial discretion; specifically, the extent to which this discretion can and should be regulated by fairly explicit formal rules. A set of rules of this kind—enunciated by the Criminal Division of the Court of Appeal—is meant to regulate the sentences imposed by the higher courts in England; there appears to be nothing comparable in any American jurisdiction, and it would be interesting to know what differences result from this.[1] Finally, it is interesting to speculate on the extent to which penal systems tend to be self-regulating, and on whether there is any sense in which they tend toward a sort of equilibrium. For example, it is conceivable that under certain conditions greater activity by the police might lead the courts to modify their sentencing policies, which might in turn affect the prison and parole systems; which might in turn affect the work of the police, and so on.

At the far end of these and other questions about the operation of penal systems lies the thorny issue of achieving an optimum policy concerning the treatment of offenders. This is a different kind of problem from those just mentioned; and it cannot really be tackled effectively without much more knowledge of the social and economic costs of different alternatives, as well as their effects. Meanwhile, the study of the working of penal systems may at least make it easier to avoid unintended consequences of changing them.

[1] Some attempts have been made in recent years, however, to devise statutory controls and/or guidelines for sentencing in the United States: see the American Law Institute's Model Penal Code, Proposed Official Draft (1962), article 7; President's Commission on Law Enforcement and Administration of Justice, Task Force Report on The Courts (1967), chap. 2, esp. pp. 14–18. See also the Standards relating to Appellate Review of Sentences, prepared by the American Bar Association project on minimum standards for criminal justice Approved Draft, 1968 (New York: 1968), esp. pp. 48–66; the Note in (1960) 69, *Yale LJ*, 1453; Robert O. Dawson, *Sentencing: The Decision as to Type, Length and Conditions of Sentence* (Boston: Little, Brown & Co., 1969), esp. chaps. 15–16.

VI

Summary and Conclusions

In conclusion, I wish to reconsider the present state of the English prison system, and in particular the general local prisons, in the light of the future developments outlined in the 1969 White Paper *People in Prison.*[1] This document describes a prison building programme which is to be carried out in the next few years; but it does more than that. In addition, it sets out the present strategy of the English prison system, and sketches a strategy for that system in the future. This strategic reassessment is not only timely; it is also far more important than the short-term plans which accompany it. The White Paper appeared at the beginning of a time of crisis for the English prison system; and it is clear that whatever happens, things are going to get worse within that system before they get better. But *People in Prison* may also mark the end, in England, of the whole penological era which began with the publication of the Gladstone report in 1895. A major objective of English penal policy during that time—indeed, the objective which more than anything else has characterized the penology of the past 75 years—has been to keep as many offenders as possible out of prison. But it is possible, even likely, that this objective is no longer realistic.

The place of imprisonment in future penal policy

We have seen that the majority of men who enter the English prison system under sentence in any year are serving fairly short sentences: even in 1968, about three-fifths of them were discharged from prison after no more than four months. The courts are in general reluctant to use imprisonment, and tend to regard it as a last resort for all but the most serious offences; as a result, only a small proportion of those sent to prison are first offenders, and the majority have been through the penal system several times previously. Though a substantial minority are entering the *prison* system for the first time,

[1] Cmnd. 4214, esp. parts V and VI.

most of the rest have been in penal institutions on a number of previous occasions.

Offenders enter the prison system through the general local prisons. Once inside these institutions, a certain fraction—the majority of men serving long sentences, and the least criminal among those serving shorter ones—are deliberately strained off, and sent to smaller and more modern institutions. During the time they are in the general local prisons, these men are merely transients, even though they may spend a substantial fraction of their sentences there before moving on. The remainder—those who stay in general locals for the whole of the time until they are returned to society—are a heterogeneous group consisting largely of fairly incompetent thieves and housebreakers, plus some men guilty of moderately serious violent crime, and a small contingent of drunkards, vagrants and minor disturbers of the peace.

In one sense, then, the men who make up the resident population of the general locals are distinguished chiefly by their inability to obtain any better conditions in which to be punished: they have been 'inside' too often, and for crimes too petty. Very few are dangerous; but they are poor candidates for 'treatment' of any kind now offered by the system, and their prospects of reform are considered bleak. They are the residue which remains when the best of the prisons' input has been skimmed of its 'star' prisoners and dangerous criminals; they are thus the *lumpen-proletariat* of the whole English penal system.

The general local prisons contain over half of the men in prison under sentence at any one time: they constitute the biggest sector of the English prison system. Indeed, as we have seen,[1] for many prisoners the general local prison *is* the English prison system. Comparatively few have ever been in an open prison, or a closed training or central prison; a large fraction have accumulated all or most of their prison experience in the 'local nick' which serves their home neighbourhoods. Yet the general local prisons are also the most neglected sector of the English penal system. In the past 25 years there have been great strides in other parts of the system: in the borstal system, in the development of open prisons, in training prisons like Wakefield and Blundeston, in the psychiatric prison at Grendon Underwood, in the newly opened industrial training prison at Coldingley. Given the very limited resources which the

[1] Above, p. 41.

English prison system had been able to command during the post-war years, it is no doubt right that the local prisons should have had a low priority during that time. But it must now be recognized that this situation cannot continue. Contrary to official estimates[1] the numbers in custody in all prison service establishments has already risen to over 40,000; and it is conceivable that by the mid-1970's there will be over 30,000 men in prison under sentence, or over half again as many as at the end of 1967.[2] On the evidence of the past fifteen years, this increase will be largely confined to the general local prisons, which already contain about one-third again as many men as they were built to hold. Plainly some action is imperative, in the near future, if a large part of the English prison system is to be prevented from returning to something like the condition in which John Howard found it.

As we have seen, longer sentences have played a part in the rise in the prison population in the last few years; and it may be that they will also cause part of the increase in the next few years. But it is important to see that the *main* factor likely to lead to an increase in the numbers in prison in England is the numbers of persons convicted of indictable offences; it is *not* the sentencing policies of the courts. Moreover, the steady increase in officially known crime and criminals, in the years since 1955, has produced a substantial number of recidivists who will continue to be at risk of imprisonment for the next 15–20 years; there is thus little reason to expect a sudden fall in the numbers of men with previous convictions passing through the courts. And it seems likely that the courts will find it difficult to postpone sending such men to prison until later in their careers than at present.

This situation is in marked contrast to that which obtained in the years up to 1930, when (as Sutherland[3] pointed out) the decline in the English prison population was due much less to a fall in the crime rate than to changes in penal policy—in particular, to the increased use of other measures in place of imprisonment. The Advisory Council on the Penal System has recently argued that '. . . [courts] themselves feel that their powers are too limited. There is a widely held view amongst sentencers that many offenders are sentenced to imprisonment, not because this is in itself the sentence

[1] See Cmnd. 4214, p. 104. [2] See Appendix C, pp. 135–136 below.
[3] E. H. Sutherland, 'The declining prison population of England' (1934), p. 24, *J. Crim. Law, Crim. & P.S.* 880; repr. in A. Cohen *et al.* (eds), *The Sutherland Papers* (Bloomington, Indiana: Indiana Univ. Press, 1956), pp. 200–226.

of choice, but, in effect, for lack of any more appropriate alternative.'[1] This may perhaps be true. But experience of the suspended sentence surely shows that there is no point in devising elaborate forms of non-custodial or 'semi-custodial' sentence as alternatives to imprisonment, unless it is clear that the courts will tend to use these for offenders who would otherwise have been imprisoned, rather than for the (much more numerous) offenders who would *not* have been imprisoned. The available evidence suggests that this is highly improbable. It seems to me to be likely, therefore, that the process of inventing new non-custodial forms of sentence for adult offenders —the 'alternatives to imprisonment' sought for so many years of this century—is just about at an end, at least in England.[2] If I am right in thinking this—if the penological era which began with the Gladstone Committee is indeed over—then a realistic approach to the treatment of offenders in the future will involve the frank recognition of the fact that a certain fraction of all convicted offenders must be sent to a penal institution for some period of time, if the other essential aims of sentencing policy are to be accomplished to any satisfactory degree. Of course in one sense this would be an undesirable outcome, since imprisonment is relatively expensive, whatever else it may be; the point is that it may nonetheless be the best outcome possible, given the objectives of the English penal system and the various constraints upon it.

If this view is accepted, it becomes imperative to re-examine the role of the short prison sentence. This measure has, of course, been almost universally execrated throughout the past seventy years, by penologists and penal reformers alike; the length of a 'short' term has steadily increased during that time, and this now seems to be interpreted as meaning any sentence of six months or less.[3] As we

[1] Advisory Council on the Penal System, Report on *Non-Custodial and Semi-Custodial Penalties* (London: HMSO, 1970), para 8. The Council recommended, *inter alia*, the use of 'community service', deferment of sentence, and various forms of 'intermittent custody', e.g. weekend imprisonment.

[2] It may have a few years left to run in the United States, however. Cf. President's Commission on Law Enforcement and Administration of Justice, Task Force report on Corrections (Washington, DC: US Government Printing Office, 1967), esp. pp. 6–10, 213–215.

[3] See. for example, the Report of the Advisory Council on the Treatment of Offenders on *Alternatives to Short Sentences of Imprisonment* (London: HMSO, 1957), esp. paras 4–8. Proposals made by the Howard League for Penal Reform, which regarded sentences of less than three months as 'short'; the Council itself considered alternatives to sentences of *six* months or less. It insisted, however, that 'the short sentence has a definite and necessary place in our criminal law'; *op. cit.*, p. 4.

have seen, the Criminal Justice Act 1967 was aimed at reducing the numbers of such sentences; and their complete abolition has often been advocated by penologists. For example, in a recent book Dr Nigel Walker argues that 'no prison sentence should be of less than six months'; and he proposes that the present sentencing structure should be replaced by one consisting of 'semi-determinate' sentences of six months to two years for those not previously imprisoned, and two to five years for those serving their second or subsequent sentences.[1] Walker concedes that the abolition of 'the short sentence' would not necessarily mean a reduction in the numbers committed to prison;[2] but he takes no account whatever of the impact of his proposals on the prison population. By way of illustration, let us assume that (1) the numbers of men committed to prison without the option of a fine remain constant at 1968 levels; (2) the effective time in prison for first-sentence men is only six months; and (3) the effective time in prison for recidivists is only two years. These are, of course, extremely conservative assumptions; even so, under Walker's scheme the prison population would rise to about 40,000, or about twice what it was in 1967–68.[3]

A usual argument against short prison sentences is that they do not provide sufficient time for 'training' or 'treatment'. This argument would have much more force, if there were any evidence at all that longer periods in penal institutions were of value for these purposes. But in fact, the available evidence—such as it is—points in exactly the opposite direction: there is nothing to suggest that long sentences are any more effective in preventing reconviction than shorter ones.[4] Even if short prison sentences were no better

[1] Nigel Walker, *Sentencing in a Rational Society* (London: Allen Lane, 1969), pp. 125–130, 193; the quotation is on p. 193. Walker also makes provision for 'precautionary' sentences for dangerous offenders, which would be longer than five years. Cf. A. E. Bottoms, 'Toward a Custodial Training Sentence for Adults', [1965] *Crim. L.R.* 582, 650, and reply by R. F. Sparks at [1966] *Crim. L.R.* 84.

[2] Walker, *op. cit.*, p. 125.

[3] If the average effective lengths are nine months and 2½ years respectively, the population would reach about 52,000; and so on. These estimates take no account of fine-defaulters, who now account for about one-third of all receptions of adult males under sentences of six months or less; Walker does not mention fine-enforcement at all.

[4] See, e.g., H. Mannheim and L. T. Wilkins, *Prediction Methods in Relation to Borstal Training* (London: HMSO, 1955), pp. 117–121; G. Benson, 'Prediction Methods and Young Prisoners' (1959), 9 *Brit. J. Delinq.* 192; C. Banks, 'Reconviction of young offenders', in G. W. Keeton and E. N. Schwarzenberger (eds), 17 *Current Legal Problems*, 61; W. H. Hammond and E. Chayen, *Persistent Criminals* (London: HMSO, 1963), chap. 11; H. Ashley Weeks, *Youthful Offenders at Highfields* (Ann Arbor, Michigan: Univ. of Michigan Press, 1958), chap. 4; P. F. C. Mueller, *Advanced Release to Parole*, Research Rept. No. 20,

than longer ones in this respect, it is obvious that they should in general be preferred, on grounds of cost.[1] There is, after all, one thing which is worse than a short period in prison followed by recidivism: and that is a long period in prison followed by recidivism. In any case, arguments about the effectiveness of short prison sentences in England must be related to the conditions in which those sentences are now served: which brings us back to the general local prisons. No doubt the short prison term will always be—to quote the recent White Paper—'an interval between two periods outside, and not the other way around';[2] but it might well be made a more productive interval than it is now. As we have seen, a term of imprisonment tends to settle the score for a fair amount of crime (in terms of additional offences, etc.) which the prisoner has committed; perhaps for this reason it has more of an impact on the offender, even now, than is commonly supposed. Certainly it cannot be said that 'treatment' in penal institutions has *failed* for most of the men now sent to prison in England; since the majority of those men, who inhabit the local prisons, have (at least in recent years) had nothing even approximating to reformative treatment.

The future of the general local prisons

The future building and investment plans announced in the 1969 White Paper give an indication of the way in which the English prison system is likely to develop, in the next decade or so. Capital investment of about £10 million is said to be planned for the year

---

California Dept. of Corrections, Sacramento, Calif. (1965); R. S. Taylor, Follow-up studies of Corrective Trainees, Part A: (London: Office of the Chief Psychologist, Prison Commission, 1960, mimeo.), pp. 19,26. An illustration of what might be accomplished by short prison sentences under better conditions than now prevail in English local prisons is provided by a Danish study carried out by Berntsen and Christiansen, in which sentences of between three and eight months were coupled with intensive in-prison social work and after-care: recidivism in an experimental group of 126 prisoners under this regime was significantly lower than that of a (roughly) comparable control group. K. Berntsen and K. O. Christiansen, 'A Resocialization Experiment with Short-Term Offenders', in *Scandinavian Studies in Criminology*, vol. 1 (London: Tavistock, 1965), pp. 35–54.

[1] There are a few offenders, of course, who are sufficiently dangerous that they must be incarcerated in order to protect the public from serious crime, especially of a violent or sexual kind. But such cases are rare; and against the slight increase in property crime which would result from a policy of reduced lengths of sentence must be weighed the cost to society of the extra incarceration involved. The *distribution* of any reduction in such costs—through more efficient schemes of compensation to victims of crime—certainly deserves consideration, however.

[2] Cmdn. 4214, para. 90.

1970–71; and higher figures are envisaged for future years.[1] So far as adult prisoners are concerned, it appears that much of this investment will go toward the provision of new medium-security institutions, most of which will be located at some distance from the larger cities. Thus, it is stated that high priority is to be given to the building of new closed prisons for Category C prisoners (that is, those not thought suitable for open prisons, but not likely escapers), serving less than eighteen months; the construction or planning of at least three more closed prisons, for Category B men, is also underway.[2] It is also hoped that by 1974 work will start on four other training prisons for men serving over eighteen months, though sites have yet to be agreed.[3] In all, the prisons for which planning has reached a fairly definite stage seem likely to provide accommodation for about 6,400 Category C prisoners and 1,000 Category B prisoners, by the middle 1970's.[4]

These new prisons will obviously ease the pressure of numbers in local prisons, though it is unlikely that they will completely eliminate overcrowding in them.[5] In addition, however, the local prisons are to receive an extensive 'refurbishing' in the next few years: improvements mentioned in the White Paper include new power supplies, some new workshops, coloured tiles on the floors, new paint, and some modification of the system of 'slopping-out' which so distresses middle-class penal reformers.[6] It is also stated that the Government has set in train a full-scale study of the design of a local prison, to be carried out by a Penal Establishments Group of the Ministry of Works. This is said to be the first study of its kind to be devoted to the special design problems of a local prison, and will include an analysis of what would be involved in the 'complete redevelopment' of one of the Victorian general local prisons.[7]

[1] Cmnd. 4214, para. 246.
[2] Ibid., para. 172.
[3] Ibid., paras 190 and 191.
[4] This includes two Category C prisons now being built, and six more which it is hoped to build in the next five years, each of which will hold 750–800 men; and the Category B prisons at Coldingley, Long Lartin and Lockwood. Cf. RPD (1968), p. 30.
[5] By the middle of the 1970's it is likely that there will be about 15,000 men in prison serving sentences of eighteen months or less, and a somewhat greater number serving longer terms. On present official estimates, about half of these men should be Category C prisoners, and 30 per cent (or about 10,000) will be in Category B. The increase in the prison population, in other words, seems likely to be about twice as great as the extra capacity announced in the White Paper.
[6] See Cmnd. 4214, paras 184–185.
[7] Ibid., para. 166.

The planned increase in training prisons will also provide an opportunity for developing new treatment methods and regimes—and for controlled experiments in evaluation of them, which has never been done up to now in English prisons.[1] The allocation policies by which inmates are selected for the institutions will be crucial, however; if the present policy of relatively indiscriminate 'skimming' of the general locals is merely continued, the situation in those prisons may well become even worse than it is now. It is also noticeable that no new open prisons are planned at present. The reason given for this is that the Criminal Justice Act 1967 has reduced the number of prisoners suitable for open conditions;[2] but as we have seen, this situation may prove to be temporary, and it is possible that there will be about 6,000 Category D prisoners (by present standards) in the system in a few years' time. According to the White Paper, the Category C prisons will have an 'effective' perimeter fence, but will not have the elaborate security precautions of the Category B institutions; prisoners will sleep in cubicles and not in secure cells, and there will be 'a degree of freedom of movement during the day'.[3] From the inmates' point of view, therefore, these institutions may approximate to the existing open prisons; and perhaps this is the best to be expected, given the concern about prison security with which the system must now contend.

Another thing which is conspicuous by its absence in these proposals, however, is any increase in the number of local prisons. Yet it can be argued that it is precisely this sector of the English prison system which most needs to increase in capacity; and that the construction of new local prisons ought to have at least as high a priority in the next decade, as the building of new training prisons. The announced 'refurbishing programme', while it would undoubtedly overcome some of the defects of existing general local prisons, really seems somewhat beside the point. The fabric of many of these buildings is—despite their age—in reasonably good condition; and they cannot, in general, be regarded as physically uncomfortable buildings (as is Dartmoor, for example), apart from the fact that they are overcrowded. This is surely the crucial problem of these institutions; even a brand-new local prison would be little

[1] Though it has been done in the borstal system: see Cmnd, 4214, p. 59.
[2] Cmnd. 4214, para. 172.
[3] Ibid.

better than the existing ones if it contained as many extra prisoners, over and above its designed capacity, as they do.

It is true that there are many things which militate against the location of new prisons in towns. Even the siting of prisons in relatively isolated rural areas raises objections from local residents; for this reason, and others, it would undoubtedly be more difficult (and expensive) to obtain suitable sites for new prisons in cities. Nonetheless, there would seem to be some strong arguments in favour of building new prisons which are 'local' in the sense of being in the cities from which most prisoners come, rather than in the rural areas in which open prisons (and the proposed new training prisons announced in the White Paper) are mainly located. *First*, as we saw in our survey of the Winson Green population,[1] the majority of the clientele of the local prisons are themselves local residents. This is especially true for the prisons in big conurbations (i.e. Birmingham, Manchester, Liverpool and London); but it is probably also true, if to a lesser extent, of smaller cities such as (in the Midlands region) Shrewsbury and Leicester. Though the prison population may display above-average geographical mobility, it nonetheless appears that the majority are local residents, who also commit their crimes locally; many retain some ties with families in the local community, and return to that community when discharged from prison. *Secondly*, given the shortness of most prisoners' sentences, it would clearly be more expedient, from a training point of view, if they could serve their sentences in one institution (as many of them do now) rather than having those sentences broken by transfer to another institution. *Thirdly*, it must be admitted that it is clearly desirable to develop specialized training regimes for particular types of prisoner, and that these will often have to be concentrated in one training prison, serving a whole region (or even the whole country). But it must surely also be admitted that at present there are very few (if any) specialized regimes which are known to be beneficial to any type of prisoner. Until more is known about the needs of particular types of prisoner, the development of new regimes can only be done on an experimental basis; and there seems little point in building special training prisons to accommodate those regimes and the men suited to them, until more is known about them. *Fourthly*, as is pointed out in the White Paper,[2] the relatively

[1] Above, pp. 33–40.
[2] *Op. cit.*, paras 187–188.

isolated rural location of many open prisons, and some closed training prisons, not only removes the prisoners from the communities in which they normally live; it also removes the prison staff, and consequently makes it difficult to recruit and keep staff at these institutions. It may also be argued that the removal of prisons and prisoners from the community into the wilderness reinforces the public's rejection of prisoners, and makes it even more difficult to re-integrate some of them into reasonably normal modes of life in their home communities.

If local prisons (that is, prisons in the local community) were not overcrowded, there would be sufficient room in them at least to begin experimenting with specialized training regimes, on a limited scale;[1] there would then be no need to invest in whole prisons devoted to, e.g. an industrial regime, until it had been tried on a smaller scale in a local prison, and seemed promising. Moreover, if the 'local' concept were more fully accepted, there would be scope for greater variety in the types of institution falling under that concept than exists at present. It might be possible at least to experiment with some types of prison which simply do not exist in England at the present day, but which could be of great value in dealing with certain types of offender. Why, for example, is there no urban open prison in England? Why should there not be prisons consisting of more or less ordinary buildings—resembling, say, a hostel, or the YMCA—in which prisoners deemed suitable for open conditions lived, while working in the community, either in prison service workshops or for commercial employers?

In fact, something like the urban open prison is already well established in this country, and elsewhere: namely, the prison hostels, 'working-out' schemes and other pre-release measures which have been used for long-sentence prisoners for a number of years now, and which it is hoped to extend in the future.[2]

It is but a short step from these hostels to the development of open prisons in the cities, in which many prisoners could serve all of their sentences, possibly after a short initial period at a closed allocation centre. There is, of course, a limit to the maximum size which any such institution could attain; and for reasons of economy of scale, and staffing, there is probably a minimum viable size as well, at

[1] Cf. the experimental regimes in special wings at Pentonville and Wandsworth—two of the worst-overcrowded prisons in England—in recent years.
[2] See Cmnd. 4214, paras 98–99.

least if the prisoners were to work on the same site (as need not be the case). But here much depends on the weight attached to security as a consideration influencing prison design. City prisons surely do not all need to be fortresses on the Pentonville model. While caution would be needed in allocating men to open prisons in cities in the early stages, it should surely be possible to acquire sufficient experience over time to keep the number of abscondings to a tolerable minimum. The proximity of such prisons to the areas from which their inmates come might help to maintain such family and other ties as they have in the community; it might also gradually promote a less rejecting attitude on the part of the general community toward prisons and prisoners, and check the tendency for prisons to become inward-looking and isolated institutions.

The argument for increasing the number of local prisons—whether open or closed—seems to me to be supported, therefore, by the evidence concerning the inputs and resident populations of those prisons. Unfortunately, however, this evidence seems to have received little consideration in the planning of the projects described in the White Paper. It is suggested at one point in that document[1] that new buildings might be built to *replace* 'the worst' of the Victorian prisons now occupying central sites in London and other cities; but there is no indication that more new prisons will be built in cities to *supplement* the older prisons. Indeed, it appears that no new urban prisons are at present planned; and the general tenor of the discussion of this subject in the White Paper suggests that none will be. It has been suggested more than once in recent years that the local prisons in city centres might even be sold by the Prison Department, and the proceeds—apart from any sum paid to the relevant local authorities—applied to the improvement of the rest of the prison system.[2] This suggestion is not mentioned in the White Paper; but it would be unwise to assume that it will not be made

[1] Ibid., para. 187.

[2] See the Eleventh Report from the Estimates Committee (Sub-Committee on Social Affairs), Session 1966–67: Prisons, Borstals and Detention Centres. (House of Commons Paper No. 599, 27 July 1967), paras 166–68, 294. A similar suggestion was in fact made early in 1967 in respect of Winson Green prison, by Mr L. G. Harris, chairman of the Margery Fry Memorial Fund: it was estimated that the site of the prison would realize £200,000 for the Birmingham City Corporation, which could be used to build a new prison outside the city. (See *The Times*, 3 February 1967.) Such a plan would, however, require legislation to amend s. 38 of the Prison Act 1952, which at present obliges the Government to offer prisons originally acquired from local authorities to those authorities at very low prices.

again in the future, with the result that the number of prisons actually located in cities would be reduced, rather than increased. This would surely be a retrograde step from a penological point of view, whatever its economic attractions. It is difficult to imagine that parallel arguments would be tolerated in respect of National Health Service hospitals, government offices or universities located in cities; yet many of these *could* be moved to rural areas, and many occupy sites at least as valuable commercially as those of urban prisons. There remains the real and important problem that the acquisition of new sites in cities is apt to be both difficult and expensive: even at present, this may take as long as seven years.[1] But if anything, this is surely an argument for retaining the present urban prisons, instead of selling them off for commercial development.

I would emphasize that I am not suggesting that political and financial control of the local prisons be returned to local authorities —as has recently been done with the English approved school system.[2] The control of crime and the treatment of prisoners is primarily the responsibility of central government, and one which local authorities are likely to be unwilling to accept; in any case, it is clear that—for reasons of security if for no other—there will always have to be *some* prisoners serving their sentences in institutions analogous to the present central prisons, which could not reasonably be provided by local authorities. The majority, however, could be dealt with in institutions which were *physically* located in urban areas.

Concerning the future role of local prisons, however, a still more important problem remains. This concerns their multi-functional nature: that is, the fact that they hold prisoners on remand, civil prisoners and fine-defaulters, as well as men sentenced to imprisonment without the option of a fine. The discussion of this problem in the White Paper is somewhat paradoxical. It is conceded that the general local prisons are trying to perform too many functions, and that in particular the task of escorting prisoners back and forth to courts often makes it impossible to provide work

[1] See Cmnd. 4214, paras 187–188.

[2] Children and Young Persons Act 1969, ss. 35–48. Nor am I suggesting that the day-to-day running of prisons should be entrusted to local authorities or 'religious or philanthropic bodies', while the Home Office remains ultimately responsible for the treatment of prisoners as well as for the cost of the system (as was suggested by Sidney and Beatrice Webb: see *English Prisons Under Local Government* (London: Longmans, 1922), pp. 245–247).

for sentenced prisoners.[1] The average working day in the general locals at present is—when the workshops are open—about three hours. Yet, having conceded this disadvantage, the White Paper states that in future local prisons should *retain* the 'trial-and-remand' function for adult male prisoners! In addition, local prisons are to continue to perform the tasks of allocation and 'categorization' of convicted prisoners, medical examination and treatment, and (at least in some cases) pre-release arrangements for long-sentence prisoners. This is especially surprising, since the White Paper appears to assume that at least *some* men—those serving 'very short sentences'—will continue to serve their sentences in local prisons, even after the new prisons envisaged in the building programme of the next few years are completed. Yet it should be plain that the 'trial-and-remand' function of local prisons is almost certain, in practice, to be incompatible with the provision of an adequate regime for men under sentence. If there is any change in the work of the general local prisons which is imperative, it is surely the *removal* of the 'trial-and-remand' function from these institutions to specially built remand centres. Indeed, the removal of men on remand from the general local prisons to remand centres would, at least until recently, have reduced those prisons' total populations by about 20 per cent; this would by itself eliminate most of the overcrowding in them.

The specialized tasks of allocation, etc., relating to men on remand and men newly sentenced, are likely to make very different demands on prison staff from the treatment of men serving even short sentences. It must also be borne in mind that the numbers on remand at any one time are unlikely to decrease much in the future. A possible solution to this problem would be to make escorts back and forth (from remand centres to the courts) the responsibility of the staff of the courts themselves. The proposals of the recent Royal Commission on Assizes and Quarter Sessions[2] for concentrating courts at fewer centres than at present, and planning sittings, will obviously help to ease the burden of escort duty on prison staff; but there seems no good reason why the staff of remand centres should not in future take over all escort work (apart from productions), including escorts back and forth to magistrates' courts. Considera-

[1] Cmnd. 4214, paras 162–165.
[2] Royal Commission on Assizes and Quarter Sessions, Report (Cmnd. 4153 of 1969), para 404.

tion might also be given to specialized institutions for fine-defaulters and civil debtors, who though they take up relatively little space in the prison system nonetheless now occupy a disproportionate amount of the time of the staff of local prisons.[1]

The changing structure of the English prison system

As new prisons are opened, and new policies implemented, the structure of the English prison system will undoubtedly change; and the relations between different types of institution may well become more complicated than they have been up to now. Indeed, there are already signs of this kind of change, such as the regionalization of the system, the introduction of parole and the new allocation policies implemented in the last few years.[2] But the prisons will presumably continue to be a system; it is highly unlikely that they will ever become a mere set of identical institutions, or that they will function independently of one another. Moreover, they will still be systematically connected to other types of penal measure, through the courts; thus they will continue to be affected by changes elsewhere in the penal system (such as those introduced by the Children and Young Persons Act 1969). It will still be important, therefore, to study these interrelationships; and to try to understand (and control) the effects which they may have on the treatment of offenders.

Consideration of this kind may lead, for example, to a reassessment of the role of prison work, and the organization of prison welfare and after-care. The extent to which profitable industrial work can be carried out in a prison depends on the input of sufficiently skilled men, and on the length of time which they remain in the institution; it may thus never be possible in some sectors of the system. (Of course, even where such work is economically possible it may be that it should be subordinated to other things, such as the reform of offenders.) Similarly, the function of welfare and after-care will depend in part on the length and nature of the prisoner's institutional experience; for the short-sentence prisoner who is a rapid recidivist, it may be best to treat the time spent in prison as an

[1] But see above, pp. 28, 33–34; it may well be that the problems of these two groups of debtors are generally quite different, and that different measures are required for each. It should also be remembered that about 10 per cent of all receptions in default of fines are (apparently) subsequently produced in court again, and given a further sentence without the option of a fine: see pp. 30–31 above.

[2] See above, pp. 12–13, 75–76.

integral part of a continuous *non*-institutional treatment programme, thus reversing the present relationship between the prison and probation services. (On the other hand, as I have already suggested, it may be best to take the opposite approach to the much-discussed idea of 'semi-detention', treating this as a species of prison sentence with liberal provisions for release on licence, rather than making it a non-institutional sentencing choice open to the courts.)

The increasing number of men serving long prison sentences in England, often for crimes of violence, is another difficult and pressing problem: it presents a dilemma from which there is no easy escape. Fortunately, the number of Category A (maximum-security) prisoners is now fairly small; it is thus possible to disperse them, fairly effectively, in five or six institutions.[1] If their numbers grow in proportion to the rest of the population in the next few years, however, the problem will become more serious; it may be that a policy of even more radical dispersal of these men, throughout all of the available Category B prisons, will be the best solution. But this will never be a possibility for the much larger number of long-sentence Category B men in prison for violent offences. To disperse these men throughout the prison system might avoid the potentially explosive consequences of concentrating them in a few institutions; but it would make it difficult, if not impossible, to develop regimes and treatment programmes suited to the nature of their criminality.[2] It would probably also result in their obtaining leadership roles in the inmate community, owing to the lengths of time they remain in prison; but to the extent that these men have a 'conscious investment in tranquillity'[3] their influence on the formal and informal systems of control in the prisons may not be a disruptive one; and there is no evidence at present which suggests that they are likely to have an adverse effect on the criminality of other inmates in the English prison system.

This last question, however—concerning the effects of relations between inmates of different types, and of the informal social system of the prison, on the prisoners' attitudes and after-conduct—is itself

[1] See Cmnd. 4214, paras 174–178; and the Report of the Sub-Committee of the Advisory Council on the Penal System, on The Regime for Long-Term Prisoners in Conditions of Maximum Security (London: HMSO, 1968), esp. pp. 13–17.

[2] Cf. above, pp. 65–67.

[3] T. and P. Morris, *Pentonville* (London: Routledge, 1963), p. 251; cf. G. M. Sykes, *The Society of Captives* (Princeton, N.J.: Princeton Univ. Press, 1958), chaps. V–VI.

one on which much more research is clearly needed, especially in England. Social relationships with other inmates, and with prison staff, make up a necessary part of the inmate's experience of imprisonment; in the present state of the English prison system, they may be one of the most important parts of that experience. Strict adherence to the time-honoured but unproven hypothesis of 'contamination', and the systematic allocation of the less criminal prisoners to selected institutions, may well mean that the remaining prisons are 'skimmed' of an important element in promoting attitude change, and are much less effective in reforming prisoners as a result. Similarly, a change from 'internal' to 'perimeter' security, by facilitating interaction among inmates, may under certain conditions make a difference to the effectiveness of institutional regimes. In any event, a change in the input or structure of the prison system may by itself produce changes in the composition of the prison population, and may thus alter quite radically the complex of factors which may influence prisoners' attitudes and after-conduct.

In respect of all of these matters, an optimum policy for the prison system must wait until a lot more research has been done. Meanwhile, what is needed (at a minimum) is an awareness of the existence of the problems, of the full range of alternative solutions, and of the different possible consequences of those alternatives. Too often, in the past, this awareness seems to have been lacking where important problems arising within the English prison and penal systems have been concerned.

Statistical Supplement

Table S.1

Previous criminality and experience of penal institutions among adult males received into prison in 1967 without the option of a fine

'urrent offence		*Previous convictions, per cent with:*						*Previous institutional sentences,* per cent with:*					
	N	*0*	*1*	*2*	*3*	*4*	*5+*	*0*	*1*	*2*	*3*	*4*	*5+*
ırder	50	32·0	14·0	2·0	14·0	8·0	30·0	58·0	14·0	4·0	2·0	6·0	16·0
ıer indictable iolence	2,080	12·7	9·1	8·1	7·9	7·1	55·2	37·9	16·2	11·3	9·9	6·4	18·4
;gery, etc.	292	24·7	15·8	12·3	7·5	4·8	34·9	49·3	15·8	9·3	5·8	6·2	13·7
pe, etc.	782	25·5	15·4	10·4	9·3	4·9	34·7	56·1	15·7	9·6	3·8	3·5	11·3
aking	7,802	3·2	4·4	5·6	7·0	7·2	72·6	20·4	15·4	13·6	12·1	8·9	29·7
;ravated ırceny	2,133	19·6	10·1	8·2	7·8	7·4	47·0	42·9	15·0	9·4	6·8	6·2	19·6
ıple larceny	7,161	4·3	4·4	5·8	5·8	6·7	73·1	21·5	15·4	12·2	9·9	7·5	33·5
:eiving	1,226	9·9	7·3	7·8	7·5	7·3	60·1	31·9	15·3	11·7	8·1	9·1	24·1
ud	1,682	16·4	9·6	8·1	7·5	6·7	51·7	36·5	17·1	8·2	6·9	6·5	24·8
ıer indictable rimes	1,074	16·1	9·5	8·0	6·6	7·5	52·2	39·3	15·2	10·3	8·4	5·3	21·5
n to ıdictable	3,244	4·31	5·2	6·4	6·7	7·4	70·0	23·3	15·6	12·4	9·6	8·1	31·0
ı-indictable	3,744	7·0	4·8	4·4	5·6	6·0	72·3	28·0	15·1	11·1	8·3	7·8	29·8
otal	31,270	8·0	6·2	6·4	6·7	6·9	65·8	27·8	15·4	11·8	9·5	7·6	27·9

Including prison, borstal, detention centre and approved school. The percentages of :eceptions having served a sentence of one of these kinds was as follows: approved ›ol, 15·2%; borstal, 21·6%; detention centre, 8·9%; prison, 63·5%. (*Source*: RPDS ›7), Table D.1.)

Table S.2. Previous criminality and penal experience of Winson Green population and receptions without option

	Population N=166 No.	%	*Receptions N=231* No.	%
Total occasions convicted:				
0	8	4·8	1	0·4
1	3	1·8	24	10·4
2	6	3·6	26	11·3
3	10	6·0	17	17·4
4	8	4·8	14	6·1
5	7	4·2	25	10·8
6–10	62	37·3	75	32·5
11–20	53	31·9	43	18·6
Over 20	9	5·4	6	2·6
Previous non-institutional measures:				
Previously on probation	106	66·3	128	55·9
Not on probation	54	33·7	101	44·1
Young offenders' institutions:				
None	89	55·6	147	63·9
1	38	23·7	41	17·8
More than 1	33	20·6	42	18·3
Previous imprisonment (without option):				
None	39	23·5	83	36·2
1	30	18·1	50	21·8
2	18	10·8	26	11·4
3	18	10·8	21	9·2
4	19	11·4	15	6·6
5	18	10·8	10	4·4
6–10	22	13·3	20	8·8
11–20	1	0·6	4	1·7
Over 20	1	0·6	—	—
Age at first conviction:				
Under 10	19	11·4	13	5·7
10–13	27	16·2	43	18·8
14–16	46	27·7	38	16·6
17–20	30	18·1	52	22·7
21–30	30	18·1	61	26·6
Over 30	14	8·4	22	9·6
Previous convictions for:				
Violence only	45	27·1	38	16·4
Sexual offences only	14	8·4	21	9·0
Both violence and sexual	4	2·4	4	1·7
Previous convictions for drunkenness:				
None	112	67·5	185	81·5
One	20	12·0	23	10·1
More than one	34	20·5	19	8·4

Table S.3. Comparisons between the short-term, medium-term and long-term residents of Winson Green, 1966

(percentages)

	Short-term (under two months) (N=53)	*Medium-term (two months–six months) (N=62)*	*Long-term (over six months) (N=52)*	*Total (N=167)*
Current offence:				
Violence	9·4	4·8	13·5	9·0
Sexual offences	3·6	1·6	3·8	3·0
Breaking offences	24·5	30·6	36·5	30·5
Robbery	—	3·2	3·8	2·4
Larceny	30·2	33·9	21·2	28·7
Fraud	3·8	4·8	9·6	5·4
Drunkenness, motoring and other offences	28·2	21·1	11·5	21·0
Previous prison sentences:				
0	46·2	14·5	11·5	23·5
1	15·4	16·1	23·1	18·1
2	15·4	8·1	9·6	10·8
3	1·9	17·7	11·5	10·8
4	5·8	16·1	11·5	11·4
5	7·7	8·1	17·3	10·8
6–10	5·8	17·7	15·4	13·3
11+	1·9	1·6	0·0	1·2
Total indictable convictions:				
0	1·9	0·0	1·9	1·2
1	7·7	1·6	0·0	3·0
2	5·8	0·0	0·0	1·8
3	11·5	6·5	1·9	6·6
4	13·5	3·2	0·0	5·4
5	1·9	4·8	0·0	2·4
6–10	26·9	27·4	9·6	21·7
11–20	13·5	22·6	42·3	25·9
21+	17·3	33·9	44·2	31·9
Total time spent in penal institutions:				
Under 6 months	50·0	17·7	7·7	24·7
6 months to 1 year	21·2	11·3	5·8	12·7
1 year to 2 years	3·8	21·0	15·4	13·9
2 years to 3 years	7·7	11·3	15·4	11·4
3 years to 4 years	1·9	12·9	13·5	9·6
4 years to 5 years	5·8	9·7	9·6	8·4
5 years to 6 years	1·9	4·8	3·8	3·6
6 years to 7 years	0·0	3·2	5·8	3·0
7 years and over	7·7	8·1	23·1	12·7

Table S.4. Discharge and transfer from Winson Green: 1966 Receptions sample

		Transferred to:		*Probability of:*				
	Dis-charged	*Open prisons*	*Closed prisons*	*Any transf.*	*Open, if transf.*	*Open (over-all)*	λ_A *(disch. vs. transf.)*	λ *Op vs clo*
Total in sample	179	107	88	·52	·55	·29	—	—
Status on reception:							·36*	·0
Without option	90	84	86	·65	·49	·29		
In default	89	23	2	·22	·92	·20		
Principal current offence:							·26*	·3
Violence (incl. robbery)	11	2	21	·68	·00	·00		
Sexual offences	2	1	8	·82	·11	·09		
Breaking offences	31	27	27	·64	·50	·32		
Larceny	42	32	16	·53	·67	·36		
Fraud	2	7	1	·80	·88	·70		
Motoring offences	17	16	5	·55	·70	·39		
Drunkenness	51	4	—	·07	1·00	·07		
Other	23	18	10	·55	·64	·35		
Total effective sentence:							·46*	·3
Not over 1 month	60	9	3	·17	·75	·13		
Over 1 month, to 3 month	69	30	3	·32	·91	·29		
Over 3 month, to 6 month	26	34	16	·65	·68	·44		
Over 6 month to 1 year	12	16	16	·73	·50	·36		
Over 1 year, to 2 year	3	14	23	·93	·38	·35		
Over 2 year, to 3 year	3	2	15	·85	·12	·10		
Over 3 year	6	2	12	·70	·14	·10		
Occasions previously convicted:							·18*	·1
None or 1	6	14	11	·81	·56	·45		
2	14	14	7	·60	·67	·40		
3	9	7	8	·63	·47	·30		
4	9	6	8	·61	·43	·26		
5	18	6	10	·47	·38	·18		
6–10	52	27	25	·50	·52	·26		
Over 10	52	14	12	·33	·54	·18		
Previous imprisonment (without option):							·26*	·2
None	44	57	32	·67	·64	·43		
1	34	13	20	·49	·39	·19		
2	23	6	6	·34	·50	·17		
3	19	3	7	·35	·30	·11		
4	12	3	5	·40	·38	·15		
5 or more	30	2	8	·25	·20	·05		
Known record of:							·09	·2
Violence	28	6	20	·48	·23	·11		
Sexual crime	8	3	12	·65	·20	·13		
Both violent and sexual	4	—	2	·33	·00	·00		
Neither	122	78	48	·51	·64	·32		

*Significant, by x^2 test, at ·01 level.

The first three columns of this table show the numbers of men in the receptions sample were discharged from Winson Green, transferred to open and to closed institutions respecti The next column shows the probabilities of being transferred to any prison; the next two show probability (as estimated from this sample) of going to an open prison if transferred, and overall (unconditional) probability of reaching an open prison. The Goodman-Kruskal stat λ_A is a measure of predictive association, indicating in this case the proportional reduction in probability of error in predicting whether or not a prisoner will be transferred, given informa about the attribute in question. A value of 1·0 would indicate perfect association in this sense, a value of zero no association. See Leo A. Goodman and Wm. H. Kruskal, 'Measures of Asso tion for cross-classification', (1954) 49 *J. Amer. Stat. Assoc.* 732–764.

Table S.5
Personal and Social Data, Winson Green population sample*

Marital status	*Living prior to reception with:* *Wife*	*Other woman*	*Parents*	*Other*	*Alone*	*Total*	*% of Total*
ried	55	9	1	1	13	79	50·0
ally separated	—	4	4	2	5	15	9·5
orced	—	3	1	1	1	6	3·8
er married	—	2	16	11	27	56	35·4
er, not known	—	—	—	1	1	2	1·3
l	55	18	22	16	47	158	100·0
f Total	34·8	11·4	13·9	10·1	29·7	100·0	

Current status	*Previous relationships:* *Married/divorced*	*Stable Common law**	*Married/divorced and Common law*	*None*	*Total*
ried	9	5	—	58	72
lly separated	—	3	1	10	14
rced	—	—	2	4	6
er married	—	8	—	45	53
r, not known	—	—	—	2	2
l	9	16	3	119	147

Of at least one year's duration.

Home until age 14	*Cause of broken home:†* *Death*	*Divorce/separation*	*Other, not known*	*Total*	*% of Total*
turally intact	—	—	—	88	67·2
natural parent alone	11	6	3	20	15·3
natural parent+step-parent	8	2	3	13	9·9
or both natural parents absent d—					
In institution	5	—	—	5	3·8
Other relatives	2	1	—	3	2·3
Other	2	—	—	2	1·5
l	28	9	6	131	100·0

Home counted as 'broken' if other than structurally intact for a period of two years or more; ct, in most such cases in this table, the home was 'broken' for four years or more.

Numbers do not total 167—the total in the sample—owing to missing data.

Table S.5 (continued):

Place of birth	*If born elsewhere, came to England at age:* <5	5–10	10–14	14–21	21+	Not known	*Total*	% T
Birmingham	—	—	—	—	—	—	42	:
Elsewhere in West Midlands	—	—	—	—	—	—	37	:
Elsewhere in England/Wales	—	—	—	—	—	—	33	
Scotland	—	—	4	5	8	4	21	
Eire	2	1	1	9	6	1	20	
Northern Ireland	2	—	—	2	—	—	4	
India, Pakistan	—	—	—	—	1	—	1	
West Indies	—	—	—	4	1	—	5	
							163	1

Father's occupation	*Highest educational attainment:* Secondary-modern or equivalent —left‡ <14/15	14/15	>14/15	Grammar school or higher	E.S.N. special school	Other	T
Professional, managerial	—	5	—	3	—	1	
Clerical, sales, etc.	2	16	3	5	2	—	
Skilled manual	3	31	5	2	1	2	
Semi-skilled manual	—	18	1	1	1	1	
Unskilled manual	—	15	5	—	—	—	
Total	5	85	14	11	4	4	

‡ '14/15' indicates school leaving age.

Prisoner's occupation: (on reception)	*Length of time in last job (or unemployed):* 1 month	1 month– 6 month	6 month– 1 year	1 year or more	*Total*	% To
Professional, managerial	—	—	—	1	1	
Clerical, sales, etc.	1	4	4	12	21	1
Skilled manual	2	5	4	12	23	1
Semi-skilled manual	3	9	4	4	20	1
Unskilled manual	9	10	3	4	26	1
Unemployed	21	23	6	8	58	3
Total	36	51	21	41	149	10

Table 36. Estimated total population of male prisoners under sentence, end-1967

Length of sentence	*Type of current offence* Murder	Other violence	Buggery etc.	Rape etc.	Breaking offences	Larceny and Receiving	Fraud	Other indict.*	All other	Total
Not over 1 month	—	4	—	1	8	48	6	1	214	282
Over 1 month, up to 3 months	—	79	3	17	293	653	76	10	807	1,858
Over 3 months, up to 6 months	—	156	22	53	722	1,283	152	38	902	3,328
Over 6 months, up to 1 year	—	244	23	95	1,179	1,198	242	145	209	3,315
Over 1 year, up to 2 years	—	607	61	204	2,467	1,332	283	390	103	5,447
Over 2 years, up to 3 years	—	462	95	163	1,287	652	197	355	29	3,240
Over 3 years, up to 4 years	—	250	66	128	460	244	95	161	9	1,393
Over 4 years, up to 5 years	—	228	63	126	324	155	94	158	8	1,126
Over 5 years, up to 7 years	—	225	64	117	206	109	51	109	2	883
Over 7 years, up to 10 years	—	159	33	48	129	19	17	85	2	492
Over 10 years (including life)	438	175	15	52	17	10	2	68	—	777
Total, all lengths of sentence	438	2,569	445	1,004	7,012	5,683	1,185	1,520	2,285	22,141
Above figures as per cent of row totals:										
Not over 1 month	—	1·4	—	0·4	2·8	17·0	2·1	0·4	75·8	100·0
Over 1 month, up to 3 months	—	4·2	0·2	0·9	11·5	35·2	4·1	0·5	43·4	100·0
Over 3 months, up to 6 months	—	4·7	0·6	1·6	21·7	38·6	4·6	1·1	27·1	100·0
Over 6 months, up to 1 year	—	6·8	0·7	2·9	35·6	36·1	7·3	4·4	6·3	100·0
Over 1 year, up to 2 years	—	11·1	1·1	3·7	45·3	24·5	5·2	7·2	1·8	100·0
Over 2 years, up to 3 years	—	14·3	2·9	5·0	39·7	20·1	6·1	11·0	1·0	100·0
Over 3 years, up to 4 years	—	17·9	4·7	9·2	33·0	16·1	6·8	11·2	0·6	100·0
Over 4 years, up to 5 years	—	20·2	5·6	11·2	28·8	13·8	5·6	14·0	0·7	100·0
Over 5 years, up to 7 years	—	25·5	7·2	13·3	23·3	12·3	5·8	12·3	0·2	100·0
Over 7 years, up to 10 years	—	32·3	6·7	9·8	26·2	7·4	3·5	17·3	0·4	100·0
Over 10 years	56·4	22·5	1·9	6·7	2·2	1·1	0·2	8·8	—	100·0
Total, all lengths of sentence	2·0	11·6	2·0	4·5	31·7	15·9	5·4	6·9	10·3	100·0

* Mostly robbery.

APPENDIX A

Mathematical Modelling of Penal Systems

Chapter II of this book sketched the structure of the English prison and penal systems; later chapters attempted to describe something of the way in which offenders tend to move through those systems, and to indicate some consequences of structural changes in the systems themselves. The next step in this kind of analysis of these systems is the construction of mathematical models of these systems, which will make possible a more precise description of the ways in which they work. This note describes the work which I am now doing in this direction; while this work is still only in the preliminary stages, a short account of the methods, problems and objectives of this kind of model-building in the penological field may be useful, in view of the small amount which has so far been done. A more detailed technical report on this research will be published elsewhere.

A 'model' in this context is simply a set of equations specifying the interrelationships between the different parts of the system being studied. In the case of the penal system, for example, the equations might describe the relations between the number of persons in the general population, and the numbers of crimes committed, persons convicted, and persons dealt with in different ways. Then, given estimates of the future population, the equations could be solved to provide corresponding estimates of the numbers of persons convicted, imprisoned, etc.; or they could be used to explore the behaviour of the system under certain hypothetical conditions. The model thus simulates, more or less closely, the behaviour of the real life system; and it can be used to analyse the internal workings of the system and its reactions to changes in its 'environment', and to aid in decision-making by showing the consequences of possible changes in the system.

Considerable work on mathematical modelling of this sort has been done in the past twenty years or so, in a variety of areas of economics and industry; in more recent times, an increasing number of attempts have been made to construct models of social systems of various kinds, and to study processes such as social mobility by mathematical methods.[1] Of particular relevance are the efforts being made by a number of researchers in different countries to develop mathematical models of educational systems.[2] There have also been a few attempts, in the United States, to construct mathematical models of penal systems. Thus, for example, an analogue computer model of the California correctional system was produced by the Space-General Corporation in 1965;[3] and a model of a hypothetical penal and judicial system was prepared by the Institute for Defense Analyses, for the President's Commission on Law Enforcement and Administration of Justice, in 1967.[4] More recently, a model of a prison and parole system has been described by Mahoney and Blozan, who have also outlined a Markov-chain approach to the study of reconviction rates;[5] I myself have suggested that this model may be useful in analysing criminal careers.[6]

It is fair to say, however, that most of the efforts made so far to produce models of whole penal or correctional systems have been of the nature of demonstration projects, aimed at illustrating the utility of mathematical modelling techniques or exploring the feasibility of applying them to penological problems. As a result, none has

[1] For a recent review of work in this field see D. J. Bartholomew, *Stochastic Models for Social Processes* (Wiley, 1967), esp. chaps. 2–3; James S. Coleman, *Introduction to Mathematical Sociology* (London: Collier-Macmillan, 1964), esp. chaps. 14,17; J. R. Lawrence (ed), *Operational Research and The Social Sciences* (London: Tavistock, 1966), parts iv and v.

[2] See, e.g., the conference papers published under the title of *Mathematical Models in Educational Planning* (OECD Education and Development Technical Reports: Paris, 1967), and references there cited; and below, n. 9.

[3] Space-General Corporation, *Prevention and Control of Crime and Delinquency*, Final report (El Monte, California: 1965), esp. pp. 220–254.

[4] President's Commission on Law Enforcement and Administration of Justice, Task Force report on *Science and Technology* (Washington, D.C.: US Government Printing Office, 1967), esp. chap 5; A. Blumstein and R. Larson, 'Models of a Total Criminal Justice System', (1969) 17, *Operations Research*, pp. 199–232.

[5] W. H. Mahoney and Carl F. Blozan, 'Cost-Benefit Evaluation of Welfare Demonstration Projects' (Bethesda, Maryland: Resources Management Corporation, 24 December 1968), chap. 6 and Appendix.

[6] In a forthcoming paper on 'A Markov Chain Model for Studying Criminal Career Patterns'. So far as I have been able to discover, there has so far been no work done in Europe on mathematical modelling of penal systems. However, there have been some limited attempts at forecasting criminality: see the papers presented at the Fourth European Conference of Directors of Criminological Research Institutes (Strasbourg: Council of Europe, 1967, mimeo.). Work is also being carried out by the Home Office on the simulation of the total Law Enforcement System in England and Wales, along the lines of the model described by Blumstein and Larson (*op. cit.*, n. 4 above). See N. Bebbington and A. McDonald, 'Research into Police Management and Control of Crime', a paper delivered at the Fourth National Conference on Research and Teaching in Criminology, Institute of Criminology, Cambridge, July 1970 (mimeo.).

produced a very realistic model of an actual penal system. Mathematically, such a model would in fact be fairly simple; while it would require an electronic computer, the computations involved are not particularly difficult. The real work involved in such model-building lies in the collection of data on population flows, crime rates, allocation policies, reconviction rates, and so forth. One possible object of this exercise, of course, is to carry out cost-effectiveness analyses; but this requires a number of assumptions about the social cost of crime, as well as further data (which are not at present available) on its economic cost.[1] The simpler objective of accurately describing a real penal system, at an informative level of detail, must in any case be accomplished first.

Fortunately, a fair amount of relevant data on the English penal system are available, from one source and another, to be used in building such a model. The official English criminal and prison statistics published by the Home Office, though inevitably not without their limitations for this purpose, are much more complete than those of many other countries (including, probably, most American jurisdictions). Computerized indices of known offenders, and of the inmates of the prison and borstal systems, are now in the process of being developed by the Home Office; these should in time provide a fairly complete picture of the movements of offenders within the institutional sub-systems. A variety of data is also available from *ad hoc* surveys on the effectiveness of particular penal measures in England, and from studies of particular types of offender which have been carried out over the past few years. The work of assembling these data is now under way; while much remains to be done, there is reason to believe that adequate information exists to make worthwhile models of the English penal system a real possibility.

The models which I am trying in the first instance to develop are Markov-chain models, based on the techniques known as input-output analysis. This technique was first developed by the economist Wassily Leontief in the 1930's, in order to study inter-industry relationships.[2] It is now widely used in economic analysis, and is a

[1] For a discussion of this see J. P. Martin, 'The Cost of Crime: some research problems', (1965) 23 *International Review of Criminal Policy*, pp. 57–63; J. P. Martin and J. Bradley, 'Design of a study of the cost of crime', (1964) 4 *Brit. J. Criminol.* 591.

[2] Wassily W. Leontief, *The Structure of the American Economy* (2nd ed., New York: Oxford University Press, 1951); W. W. Leontief *et al.*, *Studies in the*

standard tool of social accounting; and it has been used by Stone and others as the basis for demographic accounting, with special reference to the English educational system.[1] It may help to explain this technique first as it is used in economics, and then to show how it will be used in modelling the penal system.

In economic applications of input-output analysis, productive enterprises are classified into industries, each of which produces a relatively homogeneous product or group of products (its output). The output of any given industry—such as steel, coal, or textiles—may be consumed by the productive system as an intermediate input, and used in making some other good; for example, some coal is used in making steel. Or it may leave the productive system as 'final output', which is sold to consumers. Transactions in any given period of time (say, a year) between the industries making up the system can thus be set out in an *input-output table*, containing one column and one row for each industry, representing its input and output respectively. Further columns can be added to this table for the various types of final output; and extra rows are added showing payments made by industries for labour, capital, and other primary inputs from outside the industrial system. In order to contain the transactions of a whole country's economy, of course, such a table would need many rows and columns; that prepared for the United States in 1958, for example, contained eighty-one rows and columns each relating to a different industry.[2] The basic structure as such is quite simple, however. It is represented schematically on page 116.

Here the letter P designates a matrix of inter-industry transactions containing one row and column for each industry. The element at the intersection of row i and column j of this matrix shows the value of sales by industry i to industry j (which is, of course, the same as the value of purchases by industry j from industry i), in the time

---

tructure of the American Economy (New York: Oxford University Press,1953), sp. chaps. 1–3.

[1] See Richard Stone, 'A Model of the Educational System' (1965), p. 3, *Iinerva* reprinted as chap. IX of his book *Mathematics in theSocial Sciences and ther essays* (London: Chapman and Hall, 1966), pp. 104–117; *id.*, 'Input-output nd demographic accounting: a tool for demographic planning' (1966), p. 3, *Iinerva*, p. 365; 'Demographic Input-Output: An Extension of Social Acounting' (Cambridge: November 1967, mimeo.). My introduction to Professor tone's work is very considerable. A brief non-technical account is Philip edfern, 'Input-output analysis and its application to education and manpower lanning', C.A.S. Occasional Paper No. 5 (London: HMSO, 1967).

[2] The table for the United Kingdom economy now contains 35 rows and olumns, of which 27 relate to industries. See the Blue Book on National Income nd Expenditure for 1968 (London: HMSO), pp. 24–29.

period to which the tables relates. The letter f designates a column vector of final output, and the symbol n′, a row vector of primary inputs. (In practice, each of these would also be disaggregated into several columns or rows, relating to the different types of primary input and output; I have lumped them together here for the sake of simplicity.) The O at the intersection of this last row and column reflects the fact that transactions not involving some element of the industrial system are not included in the table. The column vector t and the row vector t′ contain the total outputs and inputs

Fig. A1.1

Schematic representation of static input-output table for an economy

	Industries	Rest of economy	Total
Industries	P	f	t
Rest of economy	n′	O	
Total	t′		

of the system, viz. the row and column sums, respectively, of the rest of the table; since total inputs and outputs must balance in a single time-period, these vectors are identical.

The simplest form of input-output model which can be constructed from this kind of table is a static one which assumes, first, that the total output in any time-period is wholly consumed in that time-period, either as intermediate output or as final output. In matrix notation,[1] this can be written as follows:

(1) $$t = Pi + f$$

[1] This paragraph assumes a knowledge of matrix algebra, and readers unfamiliar with it may skip the paragraph. Alternatively, they may consult, e.g. Robert McGinnis, *Mathematical Foundations for Social Analysis* (Indianapolis Bobbs Merrill, 1965), chap. 8; or G. M. Mills, *Introduction to Linear Algebra for Social Scientists* (London: Allen and Unwin, 1969).

where i designates the unit vector {1, 1 . . . 1} and so Pi designates the row sums of P. Secondly, it is assumed that each input of an industry is proportional to the total output of that industry; that is,

$$P = A\hat{t} \tag{2}$$

where A is a matrix of *technological coefficients* and $\hat{t}$ is a diagonal matrix with the elements of t on its main diagonal and zero elsewhere. The coefficients comprising the matrix A show the amounts of different inputs needed per unit of output. They may be derived from the input-output table by dividing the elements in each column of P by the corresponding element of t′, the vector of column sums. By substitution from equation (2) into equation (1), it follows that

$$\begin{aligned} t &= A\hat{t}i + f \\ &= At + f \\ &= (I - A)^{-1}f \end{aligned} \tag{3}$$

If it be assumed that the technology of the system in the future can be adequately represented by the matrix A, then given a future level of final demand f, the corresponding future level of total output t can be estimated from (3), and the corresponding future values of P and n can also be calculated.

In practice, of course, this model is too simple: in particular, the assumption that all output is consumed in the same time-period as it is produced is unrealistic, and must be replaced by some provision for time-lags in consumption. With this modification, however, much the same kind of accounting framework can be used to represent the movements of people through a social system such as the prison or penal system. The first step in modelling such a system is the construction of a table showing the transactions in one or more time-periods between different sectors of that system, and between the system and the rest of the country. Schematically such a table might be represented as shown on page 118.

The rows of this table show outflows of persons, and the columns shown inflows. The symbol Λ, known as the lag or shift operator, advances the time-period of the variable to which it is applied (by one unit, unless a higher superscript is used); similarly, Λ^{-1} retards the time period. Though the other symbols used are the same as in the preceding table, they need to be reinterpreted in their present context. The matrix designated $\Lambda^{-1}P$ is composed of as many rows and columns as there are sectors in the penal system; the *i*, *j*th element of this matrix contains the numbers of persons who were in sector *i* of the penal system at the end of last year, and are in

Fig. A1.2

Schematic representation of input-output table for penal system

		Penal system		Rest of country	Total
		this year	next year		
Penal system	last year	$\Lambda^{-1}P$		$\Lambda^{-1}f$	$\Lambda^{-1}t$
	this year		P	f	t
Rest of country		n′	$\Lambda n'$		
Total		t′	$\Lambda t'$		

sector *j* at the end of this year. (Thus, for example, the intersection of the row relating to probation and the column relating to local prisons would contain the number of persons who were on probation at the end of last year and in local prisons at the end of this year.) The same is true for the matrix P, which shows the flows of offenders from this year to next year. The row vector n′ contains the numbers entering the penal system this year from outside it (i.e. from the general population 'at risk'); the column vector f shows those leaving the system (e.g. discharged from prison) this year. The vectors t, Λ^{-1}t and Λt give the total inflows and outflows in the table, as indicated.

A table of this kind is thus a way of organizing information about the flows of persons in and out of different activities or institutional sectors in a social system, in the same way that an economic input-output table organizes information on transactions within an industrial system and between it and the rest of the economy. As with the economic table, the next step is to derive from this table a matrix of coefficients which can be used as the basis for a model. There is a difference, however, in the derivation of the coefficients used to describe the relationships between different parts of each system. In the economic model it is usually assumed that inputs are a constant proportion of outputs, so the technological matrix A is obtained by dividing the elements of P by the corresponding column sums. In demographic accounting relating to a system like the penal system, it seems better to regard outputs as a constant proportion of inputs; thus the coefficient matrix for such a system, say C, is obtained by dividing across the rows of the table by the corresponding *row* sums.[1] Thus the *i, j*th element of the transition matrix C gives the proportions of persons who were in state *i* at the beginning of the time period, who were in state *j* by the end of it.

There are several different ways in which the penal system and the different activities in it (corresponding to the industries in an economic input-output table) can be defined in a model of this kind, and the categories in the table further subdivided. The elements which move through the system are people, and the number of times they have been through the system is an important object of study; this suggests that the main classification should be numbers of previous occasions convicted.[2] In the first instance I am attempting to distinguish persons with 0, 1, 2, 3, 4, 5–10 and over 10 previous convictions, though it may prove necessary to use a somewhat coarser grouping. Then, since one object of the model is to study the relations between different penal measures, a further subdivision must be made within each category of offenders (first, second, third, etc.), between those dealt with in different ways: for example, in the case of adult offenders, being cautioned by the police, discharged, fined, put on probation, sent to prison, etc. The model is thus not concerned with *crimes* but with *persons dealt with for committing crimes*. This avoids many formidable problems concerning 'hidden' crime, changes in police activity and reporting behaviour, though of course for some purposes it might be desirable to attempt to provide for these things in the model.[3] A definitional problem arises since the model reflects transitions between states which take place in

[1] A static economic model using 'supply-determined' coefficients has in fact been proposed by A. Ghosh, in *Experiments with Input-Output Models*, University of Cambridge Department of Applied Economics Monograph No. 9 (Cambridge University Press, 1964), chap. 13.

[2] There are computational advantages in taking this as the main division, since the transition matrix then becomes block triangular. But the order of classification is arbitrary; and in practice the matrix will probably be fairly sparse in any case.

[3] Cf. The Blumstein-Larsen models, and the model described by Bebbington and McDonald, n. 4 on p. 113 above.

discrete periods of time, such as a year. Some penal measures last for varying periods of time; for example, an offender is literally in prison for a number of months or years. Other measures, such as being cautioned by the police or fined, or imprisoned for a short term, seem best regarded as events in the offender's history. To overcome this problem, the definitions of the states making up the penal system are of the form 'having *n* previous convictions, and having been dealt with by measure *j* in the most recent time-period'.[1]

In addition, then, some provision must be made for those *not* dealt with by one of the *n* measures in the most recent time-period; this can be done by explicitly defining a row and column within each category of offender for those not reconvicted, most of whom are in the general population at risk of being reconvicted at some future time. Thus, if for example, row *i* of the transition matrix C refers to those with no previous convictions who are fined in time period t_1, and column *j* relates to those with one previous conviction who are put on probation in time period t_2, the *i*, *j*th element of C is the probability of being reconvicted and put on probation in the year after having been convicted for the first time and been fined. Finally, of course, some provision must be made for those who leave the system as defined, either by death or emigration, or because they have not been reconvicted within some period of time, so that they can be regarded as 'reformed'. There exists a fair amount of evidence that almost all of those who will ever be reconvicted are reconvicted within five years.[2] Thus it seems reasonable, at least as a first approximation, to regard those who are not reconvicted within this time as effectively removed from risk of future reconviction.

The transition matrix derived from the input-output table for the penal system thus describes the structure of the system by showing the probability that an offender in any one part of the system will move to another part, or will leave the system, in a single time-period. The rows of the transition matrix C sum to less than 1·0, since in each period a proportion of those in the system leave it, either by death or emigration, or by being 'reformed'. If the distribution of

[1] Thus the model shows persons *committed* to prison, not the prison *population*. Different definitions could be used if the latter were thought more important. In this case, it would be possible to distinguish between the different types of prison—general local, special local, training, central, etc.—described in Chapter II; alternatively, and I think preferably, an entirely separate sub-model can be made of the prison system, to study movements of men within that system.

[2] See, e.g., *The Sentence of the Court* (London: HMSO, 1969), p. 65.

persons in the different states of the system at the beginning of a time-period is known, the transition matrix C makes it possible to estimate the numbers in those states at the end of the time-period. The matrix C, and the vector of initial population, together define a mathematical model of the kind known technically as an absorbing Markov chain.[1]

Thus we have the following equations, corresponding to equations (1) and (2) above:

$$t' = n' + i' \, (\Lambda^{-1}P) \tag{4}$$

$$\Lambda^{-1}P = \Lambda^{-1}\hat{t}\, C \tag{5}$$

From which it follows by substitution of (5) into (4) that

$$\begin{aligned} t' &= n' + i' \, (\Lambda^{-1}\hat{t}\, C) \\ &= n' + \Lambda^{-1} t\, C \end{aligned} \tag{6}$$

This equation says that t′, the total inflow of persons into the system in this year, is equal to n′, the new inputs from outside, plus the output of the system from last year as rearranged by the coefficient matrix C. If it is assumed that the matrix C remains constant over time, then it follows that

$$\Lambda t' = \Lambda n' + t' \, C \tag{7}$$

$$\begin{aligned} \Lambda^2 t' &= \Lambda^2 n' + \Lambda t' \, C \\ &= \Lambda^2 n' + \Lambda n' \, C + t' \, C^2 \end{aligned} \tag{8}$$

And, in general, that

$$\Lambda^{\tau} t' = \sum_{\theta=0}^{\tau-1} \Lambda_{\tau}{}^{-\theta} \, n' C^{\theta} + t' C^{\tau} \tag{9}$$

In practice, the transition matrix is unlikely to remain constant over time, even in the absence of new legislation; crime rates increase, sentencing policies change, and so forth. The equations of the system thus become slightly more complicated; but the logic of the model remains the same.[2]

Thus from estimated future inputs—in this case, estimates of the

[1] See Mahoney and Blozan, *op. cit.*, n. 5, p. 113, for a slightly different application of this model; and cf. T. Thonstad, 'A Mathematical Model of the Norwegian Educational System', in *Mathematical Models of Educational Planning*, *op. cit.*, n. 2, p. 113. A lucid introduction to this type of model is J. G. Kemeny and L. Snell, *Finite Markov Chains* (New York: Van Nostrand, 1960).

[2] See Stone, 'Input-Output and Demographic Accounting', *op. cit.*, n. 9 above, at p. 376. It should also be noted that the definitions suggested in the text mean that offenders moving from state i to j to k in one time period are treated as if they had merely moved from i to k; thus the probably small but important group of 'high-velocity' recidivists in the penal system is not clearly displayed by the model as described. There are ways of partially remedying this defect, however; see Stone, *op. cit.*, pp. 376–378.

numbers entering the general population at risk in future years—we can estimate the corresponding numbers of first, second, etc., offenders dealt with by different penal measures, the numbers still at risk and the numbers 'reformed', in those years. The usefulness of models of this kind is not confined simply to forecasting. In addition, it is possible to explore the consequences of possible changes in the system, by so to speak trying them out on the model first. New sentencing policies, for example, can be modelled by changing the appropriate elements of the transition matrix; the introduction of a new measure can be simulated by adding a new row and column to the matrix and adjusting the transition coefficients according to the ways in which the new measure may be used.

The difficult and important part of this model-building exercise, however, if the resulting model is to be of any practical or theoretical use, is the construction of the basic input-output table. No more information can be extracted from such a model than is put into it in the form of accurate data to begin with. As a first attempt, data are now being gathered together, concerning adult and juvenile male offenders convicted in England and Wales in the years 1963–67 inclusive. The number of persons convicted rose fairly steadily in those years, but the system was otherwise fairly stable structurally; and a five-year period has been chosen since, as already noted, there is reason to believe that this is long enough to give an adequate estimate of the numbers who will not be reconvicted and can thus be regarded as 'reformed'. The main categories included in the model in the first instance are number of previous occasions convicted, and type of sentence or disposition. Unfortunately the data necessary for even this crude a model are far from complete; for example, tables showing the numbers of previous proved offences of persons convicted of 'standard list' offences were last published by the Home Office in the Supplementary Criminal Statistics for 1962. Inevitably, too, many adjustments are necessary even when data are available. For example, definitions, age-groupings, and so on often do not coincide in published series of statistics; and the main tables in the published annual Criminal Statistics do not show the numbers of *persons convicted*, but the numbers of *principal convictions*, so that persons convicted more than once in the year are counted more than once. In addition, some of the data are in the form of numbers of persons; others are in the form of *rates* (e.g. of reconviction). For the latter it may prove easier to estimate directly the elements of the transition matrices and then work back to the input-output table, rather than the reverse. The only thing which can be done in these circumstances is to fill in as much of the table as possible from the available data, and then set about estimating, as far as one can, the missing parameters.

It remains to be seen how far the available data can be disaggregated so as to include other information in the model. One item of obvious importance is social class, since it is well-known that there are large differences in officially recorded criminality between different classes. Fortunately a long-term survey of a birth cohort, being carried out by Dr J. W. B. Douglas, has already provided some information on these differences;[1] as this study progresses it should give an even better picture of the differential impact of the penal system on the lives of different elements of the social system. Another factor, namely age, should possibly also be taken into consideration. But this factor seems less important in modelling the penal system than, say, the educational system. Moreover, the numbers of persons passing through the penal system in any year are much fewer than those passing through, say, the educational system; thus if the data are disaggregated too far, the numbers in some cells of the table will be too small to permit reliable estimates of the associated transition probabilities. The final categories to be used in the model must in any case depend on the data available; and it is still too early to give a final answer on this point.

Simple forecasting, and estimating the consequences of possible changes, are by no means the only uses of models of this kind in the penological field. In addition, they can facilitate the comparative analysis of penal systems. It seems likely that there are both similarities and important differences between the English penal system, for example, and the State and Federal systems in the United States;[2] comparison of the transition matrices of these systems should quickly bring out what these similarities and differences are. A further possibility is the exploration of the relations between the penal system and other aspects of the social system and the economy. Since the limits of the 'system' represented by a model of this kind

[1] J. W. B. Douglas, *et al.*, 'Delinquency and Social Class', (1966) 6 *Brit. J. Criminol.* 294.

[2] See the President's Commission on Law Enforcement and Administration of Justice, Task Force Report on *Corrections* (Washington, DC: US Government Training Office, 1967), Appendix A.

are to some extent arbitrary, they could in theory be expanded (if data were available) to include schools, mental hospitals and other institutions, and indeed the general labour force of the country. Cost-effectiveness analysis, and related decision-making about how the penal system *ought* to work, is another possibility, though this involves a rather different type of model from the one described here. But it ought perhaps to be repeated that this possibility is still very remote; and that the enthusiasm which this aspect of 'system engineering' has already generated among some penologists is premature.

APPENDIX B

Methodology of the Winson Green Surveys

The empirical data in this report, on the receptions and population of Winson Green prison, were collected in a survey carried out at that prison beginning in the autumn in 1966. Three samples of inmates were selected for the purpose of the research.

The first of these was a 10 per cent random sample of receptions into the prison. This was selected in the first instance from the prison index, by drawing every tenth index card filled out on a new reception during the year. Each prisoner is given a number in this index, when he first enters the prison (whether on remand or under sentence); and this number identifies him during that sentence, unless he is transferred to another institution. The resulting sample contained 672 inmates, as follows:

Table B.1

Composition of the 10 per cent sample of receptions into Winson Green, 1966

Adults:		
Under sentence without option	260	38·7
Fine-defaulters	114	17·0
Young Prisoners:		
Under sentence without option	15	2·2
Fine-defaulters	17	2·5
Adults on remand only	152	22·6
Boys awaiting borstal	25	3·7
Civil prisoners	48	7·1
Transferred in from other prisons	41	6·1
Total	672	99·9

It must be emphasized that the figures in this table are of receptions in 1966, and not different persons; in fact, three men (two of them fine-defaulters) are included twice in the total shown.[1]

[1] This probably understates slightly the size of the 'stage army' of vagrants, alcoholics and elderly inadequate window-smashers who enter Winson Green—and all other local prisons, especially in big cities—five to ten times a year. In

In addition to some identifying information (height, weight, Criminal Record Office file number, etc.) the index cards contain a brief description of the prisoner's offences and sentence, his movements in and out of the prison, his last address, marital status, and a little other social information. An analysis of our population sample data showed this index information to be inaccurate in some respects; in particular, it is of little value where the men's employment and marital situations are concerned.[2] For 231 of the men under sentence (including 100 fine-defaulters) we were able to obtain information about previous court appearances, from the prison, the Birmingham City Police and the Criminal Record Office at Scotland Yard; though these data are also somewhat incomplete—especially but not only in respect of minor offences—they do give a summary of the prisoners' previous criminality which is broadly consistent with that in the official Prison Department statistics.

The second of our samples was drawn from the population of 893 men incarcerated in Winson Green, or its adjacent hostel,[2] on 26 September 1966—the date on which data collection began at the prison. A 25 per cent random sample of this population was obtained, again using the prison index (the cards of men actually in the prison are kept together, and thus provide a very convenient sampling frame). This sample contained 223 men, of which 167 were under sentence for criminal offences. In terms of broad categories of prisoner, the whole sample could be compared with the

---

our research on fine-defaulters (carried on at the same time as the present study at Winson Green) we examined the index cards of *all* men received in 1966 for non-payment of a fine; in this group of 1,186 cases we found 18 men who had served three or more sentences beginning in 1966, one of them having been received into the prison eleven times.

[1] In respect of age, the index cards of our population sample were inaccurate in 16·2 per cent of the 165 cases, though seldom by more than a year. Address on reception was wrong in 21·2 per cent. For marital status and number of children, the rate of error was 14·0 per cent; the index cards showed with whom the prisoner was living in 56 per cent of all cases, in which the rate of error was 15 per cent. Place of birth was almost invariably recorded accurately. The index data on occupation were correct only 43 per cent of the time, though this figure rises to 69 per cent if the unemployed and unskilled categories are collapsed.

[2] Men in the hostel, who are serving the last few months of long sentences, are not strictly speaking a part of the population of the prison itself. Nonetheless it was felt that they should be included in the study, since this gives a fairer picture of the men under sentence in the establishment as a whole. The hostel men's records are kept with those of men in the prison; and the hostel is staffed by officers from the prison. It should also be noted that the population under study is strictly speaking the population at midnight of 26 September; it *excludes* men discharged on 26 September 1966, but *includes* men received up to midnight on that day.

population from which it was drawn, and with the average population of the prison, according to the prison's records. The results of this comparison are shown in the following table:

Table B.2

Composition of the Winson Green population on 26.9.1966, the 25 per cent sample, and the average population of the prison in 1966

	25% Sample		*26.9.1966 Population*		*Daily Average Population 1966*	
	No.	*%*	*No.*	*%*	*No.*	*%*
lults in prison under sentence:						
'Star' prisoners serving 4 years or less	30	13·5	76	8·5	54	6·4
'Ordinary' prisoners, 4 years or less	120	53·8	529	59·2	513	60·9
'Star' prisoners, >4 years	2	0·9	9	1·0	13	1·5
'Ordinary' prisoners, >4 years	10	4·5	36	4·0	30	3·6
Corrective trainees	0	0·0	0	0·0	1	0·1
Preventive detainees	3	1·3	5	0·6	3	0·4
Total adults in prison under sentence:	165	74·0	655	73·3	614	72·9
isoners in hostel	2	0·9	10	1·1	10	1·2
Total, adults under sentence:	167	74·9	665	74·4	624	74·1
vil prisoners	4	1·8	15	1·7	16	1·9
ung prisoners	3	1·3	32	3·6	35	4·2
ys awaiting Borstal allocation	16	7·2	61	6·8	39	4·6
remand:						
Awaiting trial	30	13·5	96	10·8	100	11·9
Convicted, awaiting sentence	3	1·3	24	2·7	28	3·3
Total, all types of prisoner	223	100·0	893	100·0	842	100·0

It will be seen that there are some differences between the sample and the total population from which it was selected, as revealed by the prison's records. We were told that these records might be slightly inaccurate; and the differences, over all twelve categories in the sample, do not attain statistical significance.[1] Nonetheless, it will be seen that 'star' prisoners serving shorter sentences are somewhat over-represented in our sample. It was subsequently discovered that

[1] $\chi^2_{11}=16{\cdot}2$, $\cdot20>p>\cdot10$.

five of these stars had in fact served previous prison sentences; but the sample is still slightly biassed, on the available evidence, in favour of the less criminal prisoners, a fact which had to be taken into account in interpreting some of our data.

Once the 25 per cent sample had been selected, information concerning the men under sentence was obtained from their prison records. As is well-known, administrative records of this kind are of very little value by themselves for research purposes, since they are often incomplete and the information which they do contain is of doubtful reliability. The records of our prisoners—especially those serving short sentences—were much worse than most official records in this respect. To supplement them, therefore, we also collected information from court records and (in the case of courts of assizes and quarter sessions) after-trial calendars; from prison staff, including the prison medical officer and welfare officers; and from local police forces and probation offices, and the Criminal Record Office at Scotland Yard. Finally, the men themselves were interviewed wherever possible. This was often difficult to do, in the crowded and busy conditions which prevailed in the prison during the period of the research. Moreover, some of the men were discharged, and many were transferred to other prisons, shortly after the research began. (In all, twelve prisons had to be visited, over a period of ten months, in order to complete the interviews.) Nonetheless, we managed to interview 131 of the 167 men; only fourteen, or 8·4 per cent, refused to be interviewed. Fortunately, in most of these cases information was available from other sources: the interviews were not intended to provide data of a kind which could not be obtained from records.

The third group of prisoners for whom we attempted to obtain information was a 10 per cent sample of receptions into Winson Green in the year 1963. Unfortunately, in retrospect, this part of the research design was clearly not worthwhile. The sample was randomly selected from the nominal register then in use in the prison (the present index was not introduced there until 1965). Data on these men could only be obtained from prison records; thus such information as we were able to obtain was very often incomplete. Moreover, since over half of the sample had been transferred to other prisons during their 1963 sentences, and since well over half had been re-imprisoned at least once since completing that sentence, it was an extremely difficult and time-consuming business to trace their records. Since the main object of collecting this sample was to study second and subsequent transfers, our main interest was in the 214 men who did not spend the whole of their 1963 sentences in Winson Green. But in the event, the records of 36 of this group, or about one-sixth of those transferred, could not be traced at all; we had only minimal information about these men, obtained from the nominal register, and it seems very doubtful that the remaining 178 men were an unbiassed sample. Even the limited information presented on this sample, therefore, should be treated with reserve.

The extent to which the population of Winson Green—or any other general local prison—can be regarded as typical of that sector of the English prison system is discussed briefly in Chapter II.[1] Unfortunately, because of the lack of sufficently detailed information —in particular about sentencing practices—it is impossible at present to make meaningful estimates of the relationships between the demographic and social characteristics of different parts of the country, and the inputs and populations of penal institutions. In view of certain characteristics of the Winson Green receptions and population, however, a few demographic and criminological facts about the prison's catchment area are relevant.

In 1966, Winson Green received prisoners under sentence from a total of forty-one magistrates' courts, eleven courts of quarter sessions and three assizes, located in three counties—Warwickshire, Staffordshire and Worcestershire. This area comprises, roughly speaking, the eastern half of the West Midlands Economic Planning Region. It is dominated by the Birmingham conurbation—including the boroughs of Dudley, Walsall, Wolverhampton, West Bromwich and Smethwick as well as the city of Birmingham—which had, in 1966, a total population of about 2½ million.[2] The prison's 'catchment area' also includes the industrial cities of Coventry (pop. 329,000) and Solihull (pop. 99,000).

The area as a whole has since 1951 been the fastest-growing, in terms of population, of any in England and Wales. The proportion of people of working age is higher, and the proportion of retired people lower, than in any other region; and in recent years the rate of population growth has been especially rapid in the conurbation and other urban areas. Immigration into the region played a significant part in this growth, with a net inward movement of about

[1] Above, p. 25.
[2] According to the Registrar-General's estimates, total population of the conurbation in 1966 was 2,437,100. Other figures quoted in the text are taken from the 1966 sample census (see n. 2, p. 130).

100,000 in the years 1956–64; it is estimated that over half of these migrants came from Commonwealth countries, Colonies and Protectorates, and the Irish Republic.[1] Data from the 1966 sample census indicate that in Birmingham itself there were about 52,000 persons born in Commonwealth countries, and about 57,000 born in Ireland, including 45,000 born in Eire.[2]

McClintock and Avison, in their survey of recorded crime in England and Wales in 1955–65, found that the rate of indictable offences known to the police was lower in the West Midlands conurbation than in the other five; moreover, the increase in crime in the Birmingham area (between 1955 and 1962), though substantial, was nonetheless lower than that of the other conurbations. The same was true for known offenders. In the region as a whole, however, recorded indictable offences known to the police over the decade 1955–65 increased at a slightly greater rate than in the country generally.[3] Unfortunately, insufficient data are available to permit a detailed analysis of the sentencing practices of the courts sending men to Winson Green. But figures published in the Supplementary Criminal Statistics for 1966 show that the higher courts in the police districts of Staffordshire, Warwickshire and the West Midlands imprisoned a higher proportion of all males aged 17 and over convicted in that year, than in the country as a whole—64·9 per cent, against 58·9 per cent.[4] Specifically, the fourteen higher courts

[1] Department of Economic Affairs, *The West Midlands* (London: HMSO, 1965), p. 7.

[2] General Register Office, *Sample Census 1966, England and Wales. County Report, Warwickshire* (London: HMSO, 1967), p. 7. It is known, however, that owing to errors leading to underenumeration these census figures substantially understate the proportions of coloured immigrants in Britain. It is likely that this is also true for the Irish population, which contains a high proportion of highly mobile and transient individuals, especially single men living alone in lodging-houses. For a discussion of this problem in relation to Commonwealth immigrants, see E. J. B. Rose and associates, *Colour and Citizenship* (London: Oxford University Press for the Institute of Race Relations, 1969), esp. chaps. 9–11 and appendices to part iii. 1961 Census data show that the West Midlands conurbation had a larger number of Irish-born males than any other conurbation outside London; these data also show considerable variations between different wards in Birmingham, with the central areas of Balsall Heath, Handsworth, Market Hall, Sparkbrook and Sparkhill all having over 10 per cent of residents born in Ireland. (I am indebted to Miss Ruth L. Welch of the Centre for Urban and Regional Studies at the University of Birmingham for information on this point.)

[3] F. H. McClintock and N. H. Avison, *Crime in England and Wales*, *op. cit.*, pp. 68, 134–36, 197–200, 292.

[4] Home Office, Supplementary Criminal Statistics for 1966, Group I, Tables 1 (a) and 1 (b). Magistrates' courts in these areas, however, used imprisonment slightly *less* frequently for persons 17 and over than in the country as a whole: 12·2 per cent against 12·8 per cent.

committing men to Winson Green imprisoned 847, or 47·0 per cent, of the 1,804 men convicted in 1966; the comparable percentage for all courts of assize and quarter sessions in England was 42·8.[1] It may be, therefore, that the input of Winson Green is likely to contain relatively fewer recidivists than that of other general locals in big cities in England.

[1] Ibid., Group II, Table 3.

APPENDIX C

Note on Estimation Methods

The composition of the prison population

The estimates of the population of the prison system discussed in Chapter IV were carried out in the following way. Let us designate the effective length of sentence (i.e. the time actually spent in prison) by x and y, where x is the number of whole years in the effective sentence and y is any fractional part, expressed as a proportion of one year. In the case of a fixed-term sentence with full remission, the effective length will be two-thirds of that passed by the court; e.g. for a five-year sentence $x=3$ and $y=\cdot 35$. Write P for the year-end population which it is desired to estimate, R_1 for receptions during that year, R_2 for receptions during the preceding year, R_3 for receptions in the year before that, and so on. (Define $R_0=0$.) Then for any effective length of sentence (x, y) the desired population is given approximately by

$$P^{(x,y)} = \sum_{Z=O}^{Z=X} R_z^{(x,y)} + y.\, R_{x+1}^{(x,\, y)} \qquad (R_o=o)$$

This formula is of course only an approximation; since it assumes that receptions remain at a constant level throughout each year, it will be slightly inaccurate when (as in recent years) annual receptions are increasing. However, the resultant error introduced into population estimates is in practice small; the formula has the advantage of being computationally very convenient, and is certainly good enough for the available data on prison receptions. It will be seen that in order to obtain a year-end population estimate by this method it is necessary to know, or to estimate, receptions for at least $(x+1)$ previous years. Fortunately, quite detailed statistics of receptions by length of sentence, for all types of prisoner, have been published in the Prison Department's annual reports for many years; these figures can be used to obtain a picture of the composition of the prison population by length of sentence, and as a basis for more detailed estimates by type of current offence, for later years. Statistics of receptions of males under sentence of ordinary imprisonment, for the years 1939–67, were accordingly used to make estimates of year-end populations for the years 1950–67, for eighteen groups of sentence-lengths. The groupings used in this first analysis, and the value of x and y (i.e. the estimated effective length of sentence) for each group, are shown in the following table together with the percentages of receptions of all males under sentence in 1967, in each group.

Table C.1

Estimated effective lengths of sentence in years, and percentages of receptions of males under sentence in 1967, for eighteen groups of sentence-lengths

Length of sentence	*Effective length* x	y	*Per cent of 1967 receptions*
Not over 1 week	0	·02	1·7
Over 1 week, up to 2 weeks	0	·04	3·2
Over 2 weeks, up to 5 weeks	0	·06	14·3
Over 5 weeks, up to 3 months	0	·15	27·9
Over 3 months, up to 6 months	0	·30	24·2
Over 6 months, up to 1 year	0	·61	12·0
Over 1 year, up to 18 months	1	·00	6·1
Over 18 months, up to 2 years	1	·32	4·0
Over 2 years, less than 3 years	1	·80	1·0
Three years	2	·00	2·7
Over 3 years, up to 4 years	2	·70	1·2
Over 4 years, up to 5 years	3	·40	0·8
Over 5 years, up to 7 years	4	·25	0·5
Over 7 years, up to 10 years	7	·00	0·2
Over 10 years, up to 14 years	9	·00	—*
Over 14 years (exclusive life)	12	·00	—*
Life imprisonment	10	·00	0·2
Death (commuted to life imprisonment)	10	·00	—*

These eighteen groupings are those used in the Prison Department's annual reports;[1] since the distribution of sentences within these groupings has varied slightly over the years, the average effective sentence-length in each group was estimated in the first instance from the even more detailed series of statistics of receptions published in recent years in the Supplementary Criminal Statistics.[2] A number of rather arbitrary adjustments had to be made to take into account

[1] Table C.5; see, e.g. RPDS (1967), p. 10.
[2] Table 9, Group V.

the effects of such things as loss of remission, productions, deaths, transfers to mental hospitals, fine-defaulters paying their way out of prison early, etc. The estimated effective lengths shown in the table were chosen by trial and error, so as to make the resulting estimated total population as close as possible to the published figures for the total year-end population of males under sentence; in addition, they could be checked to some extent against published figures of the prison population by length of sentence, though these are unfortunately given for only a few broad groupings which do not in general correspond to those used in the statistics of receptions.

The next step was to estimate, in the same way, the male prison population according to principal current offence. As noted in Chapter IV[1] statistics of receptions by current offence and length of sentence have been published in the Prison Department's annual reports since 1960; these were used to estimate, so far as possible, the composition of the year-end populations of males under sentence in these years. Separate estimates were made for adults and young prisoners under sentence without the option of a fine, and for fine-defaulters; and for preventive detainees and corrective trainees. (Exact figures for the total populations of the last two groups were in fact available for most of those years.) The estimated average effective lengths of sentence for the eleven groups were as follows:

Table C.2

Estimated effective lengths of sentence for eleven groups of receptions into prison without the option of a fine, 1960–67

Length of sentence	*Estimated effective length* *x*	*y*
Not over 1 month	0	·04
Over 1 month, up to 3 months	0	·15
Over 3 months, up to 6 months	0	·30
Over 6 months, up to 1 year	0	·60
Over 1 year, up to 2 years	1	·12
Over 2 years, up to 3 years	1	·94
Over 3 years, up to 4 years	2	·70
Over 4 years, up to 5 years	3	·40
Over 5 years, up to 7 years	4	·25
Over 7 years, up to 10 years	7	·00
Over 10 years	10	·00

[1] Above, pp. 59–60.

The resulting estimates, for the end of 1967, are shown in Table S.6; larceny and receiving have been combined in this table, as have all offences other than indictable ones. The next step—distributing this estimated population across the seven institutional sectors shown in Tables IV.1 and IV.2—in effect meant a seven-way partitioning of each of the 132 cells in the total estimated population (twelve offence groups, by eleven sentence-length groups), i.e. filling in a table consisting of $7 \times 11 \times 12 = 924$ cells, subject to the marginal totals for each institutional sector (estimated from the year-end total population, and the daily average populations of the institutions, as published in the Prison Department's annual report). Fortunately, of course, most of these 924 cells are empty, since it can be confidently asserted that (for example) there are no murderers, and no men serving sentences of five years or over, in open special local prisons. Nonetheless, this was an arduous process, and inevitably it was often a highly arbitrary one. As a first step, the composition of the general local prisons' population was filled in, using the Winson Green population sample as a basis; allowance was made for the apparent over-representation of star prisoners in that sample which has already been noted.[1] The rest of the population was then allocated partly by reference to the allocation policies described in Chapter II,[2] the transfer rates in our Winson Green samples and unpublished data, and partly by guesswork. I do not think that the procedure used, or the results, are wholly unreasonable; if nothing more, they can be defended as the best available at the moment. Hopefully, however, the Home Office's computerized prison index will provide exact data on the distribution of the prison population in different types of institution, in the future. Data of this kind will provide a picture of the population flows through different types of institution which will be invaluable for research purposes, as well as for operational ones.

Population forecasting

Since the system's population is a function of effective lengths of sentence and of receptions, and since receptions are in turn a function of the numbers convicted and of the sentencing policies of the courts.

[1] See above, p. 126.
[2] Above, pp. 17–20.

the size and composition, future population of the system at any time can obviously be estimated in the same way as the composition of past population, given any set of assumptions about the relevant variables. Since these may vary independently of one another, and will affect the population in different ways, it may be more accurate to estimate them separately and then compute the resulting population, than to attempt a direct projection of the latter. The main difficulty, of course, lies in estimating future trends in receptions and sentence lengths, in the next few years; in view of the legislative changes introduced by the Criminal Justice Act 1967, past trends may be of little value for this purpose. However, it seems clear that even on fairly conservative assumptions, the total population of the English prison system is likely to continue to rise sharply in the next few years, unless (as seems doubtful) there is a sudden fall in the numbers of men convicted of indictable offences. Let it be assumed, for example, that (1) the numbers of males over 17 convicted of indictable crimes continues to increase at the same rate as the average in 1960–67 (about 7 per cent per year); (2) that the probability of imprisonment for these offenders *falls* by the same rate as in 1960–67 (about 1 per cent per year); (3) that the distribution of lengths of sentences passed by the courts remains the same as in 1960–67; and that (4) 20 per cent of those becoming eligible for parole are actually released at the earliest possible opportunity. It can be estimated that on these assumptions the total population of males under sentence of imprisonment at the end of 1974 would be of the order of 30,500, compared with less than 21,000 at the end of 1968. These assumptions are deliberately oversimplified, and may prove to be inaccurate; in particular, assumption (2) ignores the substantial drop in receptions under sentence which occurred in 1968 as a result of the suspended sentence and other measures introduced in that year. As we have seen,[1] however, that reduction is likely to be much less marked in future years; it is even conceivable that receptions under sentence may *increase* in future as a result of the suspended sentence. Moreover, this measure is bound to lead to an increase in the average effective length of sentence for some prisoners. Thus assumption (2), and the population estimate based on it, may well prove to be conservative.

[1] See above, p. 83 and Table V.2.

Hypothetical effects of equal transfer rates

A final word may be said about the estimates in Chapter III[1] of the expected population of Winson Green on the hypothesis that transfer rates operated randomly for all men received regardless of current offence. If sufficient data were available, this could be calculated by treating the flow of receptions in and transfers out of the prison as a two-state continuous-time Markov process, with different transition rates for each type of prisoner received.[2] In the absence of data which would permit this calculation, I have simply divided the 'no option' men received for each current offence into two groups, by reference to the overall transfer rate (viz., 65 per cent) for 'no option' receptions; the number of men assumed *not* transferred was then weighted by the average effective length of sentence of those received for that offence, and the number assumed transferred was similarly weighted by the average time to transfer of all 'no option' receptions, which was just over one month. A similar calculation was done for fine-defaulters; and the percentage distribution by current offence of the resulting total population was treated as the percentage distribution of the stationary population, i.e. the population resulting from a constant level of receptions with a uniform probability of transfer and equal time spent in the local prison until transfer. This crude approximation neglects many things, such as productions and transfers back into the local prison; but it may suffice for the illustrative purpose for which it is intended.

[1] Above, pp. 35–36.
[2] Cf. James S. Coleman, *Introduction to Mathematical Sociology* (London: Collier-Macmillan, 1964), chaps. 4–5; D. J. Bartholomew, *Stochastic Models for Social Processes* (London: Wiley, 1967), chaps. 4–5.

APPENDIX D

Some Long-term Residents of Winson Green

It was noted in Chapter III that about one-third of our sample of the Winson Green population remained in that local prison for longer than six months; these 52 men—the 'long-term residents' of the prison—are compared with those remaining for shorter periods, in Table S.3. Of this group of 52 inmates, fifteen remained in Winson Green for over a year. As might be expected, these fifteen men tend to have longer criminal records and more extensive previous penal experience than the 37 who were in the prison between six months and a year; only one was a star prisoner, and the rest had on average over 12 previous court appearances. We have no way of knowing, at present, how typical these men are of the long-term residents of other local prisons; there is probably a fairly large element of chance involved in transfer policies concerning this type of prisoner, and the picture may well have changed somewhat since 1966, even in the West Midlands. But because of the influence within the inmate community which such men might conceivably exercise in view of their relatively long stays in the prison, a brief description of them may be of interest.

These 15 inmates are a heterogeneous group, and our data indicate that a number of different factors were responsible for their comparatively lengthy periods of residence in the general local prison. About a third of the group spent such long periods in Winson Green for more or less accidental reasons. One man was kept there because of ill health:

Case No. 131. Aged 63, serving two years for 10 charges of false pretences. Convicted on thirteen occasions since the age of 33, he had served eight prison terms of two years or less, all for larceny, false pretences or forgery. He claimed that he stole to pay for hotel rooms, which were more comfortable than hostels. He had no criminal associates. He had been in hospital several times with carcinoma of the bladder, and was too ill to work; and he spent most of this sentence in the Winson Green hospital and in a general hospital in the city. 'I've always been treated well in prison, because I've always been in the hospital.' During this sentence he was reconciled with his wife, from whom he had been separated for many years, and was planning to return with her after being discharged.

Three others were in fact transferred to other prisons, but were later returned to Winson Green and thus spent the majority of their terms there. One of these men was transferred to Ashwell open prison after 16 months, came down with pneumonia while on home leave from that prison, and was returned to Winson Green for the last two months of his sentence; another was transferred to Sudbury open prison after nine months, absconded and was returned to Winson Green after having been at large for one day. The third was the only prisoner in this group with a history of previous absconding:

Case No. 157. Aged 27, serving four years for false pretences and larceny. He had stolen a cheque book from a hotel room, and passed cheques totalling over £150; this was his usual type of crime, and he had nearly 100 known offences in all, at eleven previous court appearances. He had served five previous prison sentences, including three years' corrective training; his average time at liberty since the age of 17 was about four months. Previously married and divorced, he was now married to a woman with whom he had lived for several years; they had four children. He claimed to have no criminal friends or associates, committed his crimes alone, and came from a family in which no other member had been delinquent.

He was classified as unsuitable for an open prison, presumably because he had absconded from Sudbury, and had also failed to return from home leave, during his corrective training sentence. He was offered transfer to the closed training prison at Nottingham, but refused this; subsequently he was transferred to the closed special local prison at Stafford, after having spent fifteen months in Winson Green. He absconded from Stafford the same day, was promptly recaptured and returned to Winson Green to complete his term.

Three other men in the group were eventually transferred to other closed prisons after spending more than a year in Winson Green, and were apparently not returned to the general local prison. These men might have been transferred sooner, if more accommodation had been available in closed training or central prisons. As the following rather pathetic case shows, however, selection for training prisons was not invariably based on clear criteria of 'trainability' at the time of our survey:

> *Case No. 153.* Aged 33, he was serving three years for housebeaking and theft of property worth £115. His criminal record began at age eight, and included nine previous court appearances, all for housebreaking and larceny; he had done three years' corrective training and five other prison sentences, including one of five years and one of seven. In all, he had spent over 11 years in penal institutions, as well as eight years in an ESN school; his average time at liberty was four months. His IQ was 70, and according to police records all of his crimes had been very simple and relatively trivial ones. Unmarried, he denied having any close acquaintances who were criminals.
>
> Early in 1967, according to prison hospital records, this man began to complain that his insides were rotten, and that he was giving off unpleasant odours which the other prisoners detected and talked about. These complaints were diagnosed as evidence of paranoïd schizophrenia, and he was given electro-convulsive therapy and drug treatment. By June 1967 he was still undergoing treatment, though he was said to be 'responding'; in August of that year, after spending sixteen months in Winson Green, he was transferred to the training prison at Gartree, on one of the bulk transfers by which that prison was filled in the first instance.

Finally, one man was transferred *into* Winson Green after having started his sentence in another local prison:

> *Case No. 4.* Aged 39, serving four years for housebreaking. Since the age of 11 he had appeared in court on 13 occasions, mostly for stealing and breaking offences of a fairly trivial kind; he had, however, served four years for causing grievous bodily harm (in a grudge fight), in addition to six other prison sentences. His father and two brothers also had convictions, and he himself had many criminal acquaintances. He had never married, and always lived alone, usually in lodging houses, since first leaving home.
>
> All of his previous sentences had been served in local prisons, including two in Winson Green. On this sentence he had assaulted a prison officer in his first prison, and was transferred for this reason; he had asked to come to Winson Green. He did not associate at all with other prisoners, and even worked by himself (sewing mailbags in his cell); asked what he thought was the

worst thing about being in prison he could find no complaint, and declared 'It's better now than it ever was.'

He spent 889 days in Winson Green, out of a total of 1,255 in his sentence.

The remaining seven men, who spent all of their sentences in Winson Green, were mostly serving shorter sentences than the men just described; with one exception, they were doing eighteen-month or two-year terms, and so spent between twelve and fifteen months in the general local prison, after deducting remission for good conduct. One of these men was a 'star' prisoner; the rest had on average thirteen previous court appearances and four previous prison sentences, and it is interesting to note that all of their previous sentences (of which the longest had been three years) were served entirely in local prisons. The following two cases are fairly typical of this group:

Case No. 115. Aged 34, serving 18 months for shopbreaking. His record included eighteen court appearances since the age of sixteen, all for theft and breaking offences; he had been in borstal, and served nine previous prison sentences of up to three years, all in local prisons. He had a brother with a criminal record, and admitted to several criminal acquaintances, but described himself as 'not much for company—a loner' when asked about friends in prison. He was unmarried.

After four months, he was picked for transfer to Ashwell open prison, but for some reason it was not possible for him to be transferred at that time. Two months later he was interviewed by the governor of another open training prison, who did not regard him as suitable for transfer; so the prisoner asked not to be considered again for transfer. He spent just over a year in Winson Green.

Case No. 74. Aged 22, he was serving three years on four charges of larceny, with 210 offences taken into consideration. Most of these were thefts from motor cars, committed on what appeared to be mainly joyriding episodes. He had been convicted on ten previous occasions, including once for robbery and wounding, and once for indecent assault; he had been in approved school and borstal, and had had one previous prison sentence. Though married, he had been living apart from his wife before beginning this sentence. Classified as suitable for a closed prison, he was apparently never considered for transfer.

Three of this group were classified on reception into Winson Green as suitable for open prisons. As Case No. 115 illustrates, however, this initial classification by no means guaranteed allocation to an open institution.

It was argued in Chapter II that because of conditions in the general local prisons, and the short sentences of the majority of their inmates, it is unlikely that there is a well-developed inmate social system in those institutions, at least in comparison with training or central prisons. However similar the attitudes and values of the general locals' inmates may be, some amount of continued association between such inmates is presumably necessary before stable relationships of any kind can develop between them. If such relationships do exist in general local prisons, it seems reasonable to assume that they will be most marked among the 'long-term' residents; and that those men spending as long as a year in the institution would have the greatest access to leadership and other roles or positions of importance in the inmate community.

Unfortunately, we were not able to investigate relationships among the inmates of Winson Green, or between inmates and staff; thus we have no direct evidence on the social roles which these 15 men might have occupied while they were in the prison. The most we can do is to consider how far they possess attributes which might lead them to have high status in the eyes of other prisoners, or to occupy distinctive positions in the social structure of the prison. Our data on this point must be interpreted with care. But if any generalization can be made on the basis of our limited information, it is surely that none of the 15 conforms very closely to the traditional picture of leadership or high status in the inmate community.[1] Five of the 15 could perhaps be described, on the available evidence, as integrated to some degree with a criminal sub-culture outside the prison. One of these men was Case No. 4, already described; two other clear examples are the following:

Case No. 148. Aged 26, serving 2½ years for assault occasioning actual bodily harm and wounding, during a fight in a pub, also for assault on a police constable, and causing death by dangerous driving. Convicted on fourteen previous occasions since the age of ten, he had been in approved school and borstal, and had served four previous prison sentences, all but one of them in Winson Green: his record included a conviction for manslaughter

[1] Cf. the references on p. 48 above, n. 4.

while in the Army (a result of another pub fight), and another charge of occasioning actual bodily harm, as well as convictions for theft and housebreaking. Married and in the process of being divorced, he had been living in an apparently stable common-law liaison for over four years. He admitted to having a number of criminal friends in Winson Green and on the outside; he had one brother who had also been in approved school and in prison.

He was transferred to a closed training prison after spending fourteen months in Winson Green.

Case No. 167. Aged 43, serving eight years' preventive detention after conviction of warehousebreaking and attempted theft of goods worth over £10,000. This man was a member of a well-known criminal family living in the West Midlands, of whom it was said that at least one member has been in Winson Green prison since it was opened in 1849. Seventeen previous court appearances included convictions for breaking offences, theft, drunkenness and assault; during one burglary he had accidentally killed a man, and served ten years for manslaughter. Married but divorced just before this sentence, he admitted close connections with many other full-time criminals in London and in the Birmingham area. But he could not be described as a successful professional criminal: he had spent a total of twelve years in penal institutions, and his average time at liberty between sentences was under ten months. He was said to be of subnormal intelligence.

Understandably described as a 'poor prospect' for reform, he spent just over a year in Winson Green before being transferred to a central prison for the rest of his sentence.

But while these men were fairly clearly committed to a criminal way of life, none of them—indeed none of the whole group—was a successful criminal by any reasonable criteria. Only one inmate (No. 148) had a record of serious violence. The remainder included one man with no previous prison experience; a group of incompetent petty burglars; and four false pretenders whose careers—exemplified by case No. 157—strikingly resembled the pattern of 'systematic check forgery' described by Lemert.[1] The majority admitted to no close friends who were criminals, were not known to have criminal

[1] E. Lemert, 'The Systematic Check Forger', (1958) 6 *Social Problems*, 141. It might be expected that these men, when in prison, would approximate to the 'con politician' type described by Schrag, or the 'merchant' or 'centre man' described by Sykes. There was some evidence of this in the case of one man, who had worked in the prison kitchen until he was caught stealing food. But there was no such evidence in the case of the other three men, one of whom (No. 131) was the elderly man who remained in Winson Green because of illness.

associates, and appear to have committed the majority of their crimes alone. The two who apparently had the most extensive associations with other criminals (Nos. 4 and 115) were isolates who had no apparent contact with other prisoners.

In summary, then, the inmates spending the longest time in Winson Green were a miscellaneous group of men, whose comparatively lengthy periods of residence in the general local were due to several different factors. Whatever the inmate social system of Winson Green may have been like at the time of our survey, it seems unlikely to have centred on these men, despite the time they spent in that prison.

Index